The Christian

Affirmation

The Christian Affirmation

by

John Dalrymple

DIMENSION BOOKS
Denville, New Jersey
DARTON, LONGMAN & TODD
London

Inquiries should be sent to the publishers,
DARTON, LONGMAN & TODD LIMITED
85 GLOUCESTER ROAD, LONDON SW7 4SU

and

DIMENSION BOOKS
DENVILLE, NEW JERSEY
and not to the printers

First published 1971

© 1971 John Dalrymple

ISBN 0 232 51162 4

Printed in Great Britain by
Fletcher & Son Ltd, Norwich

CONTENTS

CHAPTER ONE

Christian Life is an Affirmation

This is a book about basic attitudes, about what is traditionally called the spiritual life. The word spirituality today is understandably suspect because of the sad incidence among christians of the practice of escaping from public responsibilities by retiring into a private world labelled spiritual life. This rightly repels those who have read the gospels and want to follow Jesus Christ, so it is perhaps preferable to talk about basic attitudes to living rather than about the spiritual life, although the word spiritual is in fact a good one to describe what is meant by basic attitude. In all we do we manifest a fundamental attitude to living. We show, by the way we respond to the morning alarm clock or the way we meet people, the attitude which governs our life. Those of us who are mature, in the sense of being formed characters and not adolescents on the way to being formed, manifest a basic attitude to life which is constant. We are not always changing our fundamental responses. They remain the same, even though we do not always in individual cases act faithfully towards them. We are sufficiently formed to be able to be identified as someone with a constant fundamental attitude. This is what is meant by saying we are persons. Spirituality is about this fundamental way of being a person. It is concerned not chiefly with the transient reactions of this and that moment, but with our underlying approach to life which is the source of the reactions of the passing moment. Spirituality is thus paradoxically both in and out of the passing moment, both on the surface and not on the surface of living. This is what makes it difficult to introduce without giving the wrong impression.

The basic christian attitude to living may be summed up by saying that it is a threefold commitment, at each stage of which we are summoned by Christ to respond affirmatively, to say yes. It is a commitment to life, to people and to society. First we are asked to say yes to life. This means reacting to the successive challenges of life creatively, in a cooperative outgoing manner. Our instinct is often to withdraw into ourselves and refuse the challenge that a situation brings — this is to say no to life, and is the opposite of the christian attitude which is creative and co-operative. This saying yes or no to life occurs in every situation, from the ordinary ones like getting out of bed in the morning or opening unpleasant looking letters to the big decisive moments like applying for a job or facing a family crisis. In all these situations we can either respond affirmatively by facing the challenge and thus manifest a basic attitude which corresponds to words like accept, face up to, engage, be involved in, be positive, be creative, or we can react negatively and withdraw from the situation, thus exhibiting an attitude for which words like refuse, postpone, escape, put aside, are apt.

Two things should be noted about this question of basic attitudes. The first is the inner connection between the big and the little responses: if we, for instance, continually say no in the small events of life we are likely to fail at the crucial moments when big issues are at stake. This is an important truth, for it underlines how our attitude to life is a continuous thing which grows or diminishes

11

from situation to situation and which can never be put in cold storage to be used when needed. Our attitude to life is after all *ourselves*, and only ceases when we cease. We cannot kid ourselves that deep down we are different from our everyday selves, because our everyday selves are our real selves. The second point to note is that according to whether we say yes or no to the successive situations of life, we grow or diminish as persons. There is no standing still; we either expand or contract as personalities and this expansion or contraction depends on us, on whether we meet courageously or withdraw timorously from the challenges of living. In a very real sense we "make" our personalities and have ourselves to blame if we grow into withdrawn, narrow persons who are constantly running away from life, just as it is because we have faced up to life in the past that we become developed, real outgoing persons in the present.

It is the meaning of the gospel taught and lived by Jesus Christ that men must have the attitude of saying yes to the succeeding situations of life and never turn in on themselves and say no. Turning in on self, saying no to life, is the attitude which is at the root of all the sins against Christ's teaching, like uncharity and pride, and the less-than-christian responses like postponing decisions and brushing difficult knowledge away from our conscious minds. All these latter responses are forms of repression, equivalent ways of saying no to life by putting off the decision to say yes. Putting off the decision to say yes is often more harmful to the character than saying no outright, for life does not wait for us. If we are not going forward to meet each situation creatively, we are going backwards. There is either growth or diminishment, no third option.

In the second place we are asked to say yes to people. Saying yes to life mostly involves saying yes to people, for we live surrounded by people and even when alone we are usually either preparing for our next meeting with people or mulling over our last meeting. Even our private moments are public in intention. The christian attitude to life, then, is one of affirmative, cooperative engagement towards our fellow men in the situations that bring them into our life. This means saying yes to people in a thoroughly open-ended way. We cannot initially say yes and then withdraw if we find things too uncomfortable for us. The first yes involves from the start the christian intention to go all the way with our neighbor. Thus the telephone samaritan who says "yes, come round immediately" knows that the initial yes will lead to a series of unforeseeable further yeses which will cost all the time, trouble, anxiety and loss of independence that becoming involved in another human being inevitably brings. On the other hand, saying yes in this way is clearly not being a yes-man in the colloquial sense of the term, for the yes-man is in fact one who says no to life under the guise of saying yes, one who chooses the easy option because it is less trouble. In the true sense, saying yes to people means entering into an engagement with them, relating to them positively and creatively, willing to share time and privacy with them — in which sharing there may often be occasions when we have to say no in order to remain helpful and creative towards them, as every mother and father knows.

It is always possible to turn away from people who intrude into our lives and this refusal to be affirmative is often disguised. Professed christians seldom explicitly exclude people from their love, for that would be too obviously unchristian, but there are a number of equivalent ways of saying no, passing by on the other side of the road because we are too busy to stop. We say no in two ways, consciously and explicitly by saying we are not going to help — these are our sins of uncharity, laziness, carelessness, malice, selfishness, unconsciously and implicitly by accepting without question all the built-in barriers to social and personal life which our less-than-christian society imposes on us. These barriers are the barriers of class, creed, race, color, even politics, with which our individual lives are fenced around. They in turn are thrown up by the deep-seated urge in man to remain alone and apart within a controllable community and not be drawn into relations with "outsiders." How many christians in this country passively accept these fences as given and do nothing to abolish them, settling for living their christian lives within barriers laid down by the status quo rather than making their christian lives precisely the breaking through and down of those barriers? Saying yes to people means breaking through these barriers by loving through them. (They will be broken down by loving through them more effectively than by violence without love.) Loving across these gaps is not easy because it means going against inherited social taboos and doing things like having the unwashed and smelly into one's house, allowing one's daughter to meet colored men, being seen as a priest with scandalous people, and doing this with love and not merely out of a desire to shock the less adventurous.

By the way we handle our relationships with people we either grow or diminish as persons. "Through the Thou a man becomes I" (Buber). This means for everybody accepting the challenge of breaking out of the shell in which we are born and develop, with its conscious and unconscious layers noted above. There can be no growth without some breaking out. Sooner or later for everyone there is the decision to say yes and leave behind the security of past patterns and walk out into the unknown. Not to do so when the moment comes is to say no to life and people, and so diminish. A key part in this transformation is played by human passion. It is the God-given catalyst which allows the transformation to take place. Although it is superseded by a deeper transformation, without it the necessary energy for bold action would be lacking. The result of this act is the achievement of "personal" living, that is, life lived truly authentically, no longer according to patterns laid down by teaching from outside, or behind masks thrown up by ourselves for our protection and inner security, but from within, from the newly discovered center of our true, unmasked self. It means meeting people and treating them as people in their own right and no longer as "opponents" or threats to oneself. It means, in other words, loving them and centering upon them, away from self.

In the third place we are asked to say yes to society. For long we have been giving assent to the truth that man is a social being with duties to society, but it is especially in this generation that christians are being led to realize that their christian commitment to society means not only trying to live an individually christian life in secular society but trying to make that society christian. It is one thing, and an important one, to aim at personal christianity and to sanctify one's relationships with other people, as we have noted. But that is not enough, because of this very need for commitment to society itself. This means relating to society politically and doing so in a christian way. It means being politically christian. Clearly this does not necessarily mean going into politics. What is meant is that because christianity is social, and therefore salvation in part political, the real christian must say yes to being socially and politically committed. He cannot opt out of influencing the way society is formed and governed, least of all in a democracy.

Ultimately the social principles of christianity are aiming at unity throughout the world. Jesus died "to gather together in unity the scattered children of God" (John 11:52). Both in the world-wide field and in the society we live in, therefore, we have to aim at melting all those barriers which militate against unity among men, the barriers of class, creed, race, color being the most obvious. Being a good christian, for instance, does not mean accepting the class system of this country with its less than christian separation of people into privileged and unprivileged, and trying to be christian within it. It means doing one's best to abolish privileges which are based on birth or unearned wealth, and the best way to start this is personally to live as if they did not exist. But having started, one should not rest there. As has been noted, for instance, the colored people imprisoned in the ghettos of American cities do not ask for friendly jailers to ameliorate life in the slums by running youth clubs and social services, but for liberation from those slums. Saying yes to society means a christian change of heart, but a change of heart which issues forth in christian social action, not just personal adjustment to a less-than-christian system. To tolerate an unjust society in any way is to nullify personal spirituality. Saying yes to people must be accompanied by saying yes to society, if it is not to become an ivory tower occupation. In other words, spirituality is communal and public at the same time as it is intensely personal and private. This is what is meant by saying that the christian task is a threefold commitment, not three commitments. We cannot choose between saying yes to life, people or society, because saying yes to one implies saying yes to the others. There is a profound unity in human living, which only the analytical, limited mind of man divides into separate compartments. In reality we say yes or no to the whole of human living every time we react to a particular situation.

When we say yes to life, people and society, whom are we ultimately saying yes to? It is the christian revelation that the answer to that question is God the Father. Christ came to tell us that the fundamental reality of our lives, the ultimate ground of our existence, in which we live and move and have our being, is Father. Behind all the events of our lives, watching over us, caring for us, counting the number of hairs on our head, knowing when the sparrow falls to the ground, is the loving concern of the Father. God is not a remote being far away and separate from this world, who knows us from an infinite distance, but the very energy we live by, a divine field of force in which we operate, which is at the same time supremely personal and, according to Jesus, fatherly. This means that the events of life, our meetings with people, the social situations we find ourselves in, are watched and planned and sent by God who permeates our history from within, so that we could call everything that happens to us the fringe of his garment which we either reach out to touch (say yes) or hold back from (say no). Teilhard called matter Jacob's Ladder by which we mount up to heaven, and an earlier Jesuit called the events of our lives sacraments of the present moment. It is the same insight — the realization that God is present within our lives, and therefore the responses we make to the challenges of life are personal responses to God. There is no escaping from him or exiling him innocuously to heaven. Each event of life is his clear call to us, personal and urgent, here and now, and each response we make has an opportunity of becoming the "spiritual sacrifice" which St. Paul and the Early Church saw as the basis of all christian living (cf Romans 12:1).

It now becomes clear that for the christian the threefold commitment of life is fundamentally a commitment to God. This means that everyday christian living can be made into prayer. We say *can be* rather than *is* because it depends on the individual response, on whether we intentionally say yes or no to God in the event concerned. How is this done? By simply realizing that when we say yes to life, people and society, we are deep down also saying yes to God, or rather not *also* saying yes as if God were still separate from the events of life, but saying yes to God within the events of life. Thus getting out of bed in the morning is not just facing life but facing God, and opening difficult letters courageously is facing the Father whose providence knows about the letter and into whose mysterious plan it falls. Even more, our relationships to people, both the ones who excite and please us and the ones we find it difficult to love, are relationships to God. We have Christ's graphic word for this in his description of the Judgment, so that there is now excuse for us to say but *when* did we see you as colored immigrant or as a down-and-out and not bother about you, Lord? Likewise, our political action for the betterment of society is also an encounter with God, not only in the sense that God is in society but also in the sense that he is in *us*, and our actions within the secular world are joint actions with him for the progress of humanity. The signs of the kingdom in Jesus' day were the healing of the sick, the liberating of the imprisoned and the preaching of the good news to poor people, and these signs should still be present in our day through our efforts. By participating in this continuing redeeming activity of Christ in society and making it happen, the christian ensures that the signs of the kingdom are still in this world. Such christian action in the secular world is prayer, for it is saying yes to God's will for society, and making it come about. This is a creative yes which brings events about, like our Lady's fiat at the Annunciation; it is not a passive one which merely submits to events beyond control. (It is also, like Mary's yes, open-ended to the future, cancelling all possible limiting conditions and escape clauses.)

Seen in this way, life not only becomes a prayer, but the whole of life becomes a prayer. There is now no action which cannot be made into a prayer, because God is present in every corner of man's life. Man's commitment to himself, to other people and to society, is also never ending and has no gaps. This is no new truth. It is found in the New Testament with St. Paul's injunction to pray without ceasing, and was part of the Jewish consciousness of the closeness of Yahweh to his Chosen People. The point is to make these encounters real meetings with God, and not just give lip service to the theoretical truth. It is, after all, one thing to talk about the presence of God everywhere in the sacrament of the present moment, but quite another to live as if this astonishing thing were true. Perhaps too many people today speak glibly of life being a prayer. The witness God asks in the modern world is chiefly the witness of actions, not words, since words cost little when they are unaccompanied by deeds. The christian word has always been meant to be an event as well as a sound from the mouth, and the really convincing christian today is the man whose life shows forth the Truth that God is in it, and who can show his neighbors with more than words that he is encountering God in day-to-day living.

CHAPTER TWO

The Risk of Loving

Man's understanding of himself has developed in the modern age. A hundred years ago, if you said "person" you conjured up the image of *separateness*. Words like "sovereignty" and "inalienable" rose to the lips. Man was thought of primarily as an individual with rights of his own, an island in a sea of islands. But now we understand things differently. Without denying the inalienability and essential separateness of a person, we think it equally necessary to stress that he is only a person because he can enter into relations with other persons; that, as well as existing for himself he exists for other people; that "the most vital core of a man does not consist in the solitary affirmation of his individual autonomy, but in availability, welcome, receptivity" (Moeller). In fact that man is *not* an island but part of the main, and that the defining element in man, which distinguishes him from inanimate beings, is his ability to know himself and enter into spiritual contact with other persons. Man's humanity essentially consists in this ability to open out to people and welcome them into his life.

Once it is agreed that what makes a man a person is his entering into relationships with other persons, it can be seen that the notion of personality admits of degrees. One can become more or less a person because one can have more or less contact with other people and enter into deep or shallow relations with them. The more complete person is precisely he who has entered into deep relations with his fellow men, and the shallow person is the man who has held back from this. "The more really special a thing is, the more abundance of being it has in itself, the more intimate unity and mutual participation there will be between it and what is other than itself," says Karl Rahner. Psychologists of all schools are agreed that the realization of a man's personality comes about by relating well and healthily to other men and not by remaining solitary. There is an endless variety and endless amount of ways in which a man can enter into relationships with the persons who surround his life, and therefore there are endless possibilities of development for one individual person. He can remain relatively undeveloped as a person by remaining isolated, or he can grow into the rich and varied relationships with his fellow men. Martin Buber's aphorism that "through the Thou a man becomes I" is apt here. We do not exist as static, unchanging individuals and merely grow old as the years pass by; we *become* ourselves with the passing years and either grow or diminish according as we have allowed our personalities to be opened up by the experience of love. Perhaps the most interesting aspect of these ideas is that it depends on the individual himself to become himself; the growth of the person I am meant to be is voluntary on my part. It depends to a great extent on how much I have allowed other people to become "thou's" in my life whether I grow into the person I am destined to be, or stay a stunted growth all my life.

Now, if we human beings grow by the way we relate to other people, we should give some thought to this process in our lives. It is not an automatic process. Just to be physically in the company of other human beings means nothing. We do it, for instance, most days in public transportation. Other people may be highly complicated personalities with rich histories of their own, but to us, as they bump around and step on our toes in the underground, they are no more than objects who occupy the space next to us. We do not treat them as persons at all, but prefer to stand silently beside them waiting for the end of the journey, which brings release, and communication with the real persons in our lives at home. On the other hand, if we trouble to speak to our neighbors in the train (or waiters in the restaurant) the relationship becomes quite different. We begin, very tentatively, to know them. We thus begin to regard them not only as objects occupying space beside us, but as subjects, people to speak to and share the journey with. We have begun to enter into personal dialogue with them. A real relationship has sprung up between us. When this happens, it does not happen automatically, but by mutual consent. As has already been said, one enters into personal dialogue with people by choice. An act of the will begins it.

It can prove a rewarding study to pursue the process of dialogue through the stages of acquaintance to companionship to friendship and finally to love. There is, for instance,

an important period when the surface acquaintance gives way to friendship and both
partners suddenly begin to enter one another's lives; the friendship becomes an interior
one; they begin to *communicate*. So, too,
the last stage of love, if reached, is important,
when the barriers have gone and mutual
availability is almost complete. But the point
to note, once again, is that this is a voluntary
process. At any given moment a man can call
a halt and, as it were, step off the escalator.
We do this all the time. We do not admit
many to the intimacies of deep friendship,
let alone love. Some people even find it difficult (or are unwilling) to make that initial
step which turns the other from an "it" into
a "thou." Nevertheless most of us are aware
that there is a deep need in us to love and
be loved and that therefore we are only answering an instinctive natural call when we
set in motion the process whereby we form
friendships and take the risks involved in
love.

A further question needs to be answered.
What is it that holds men back from entering into real relationships? What makes them
erect barriers of privacy round their personalities and a whole array of "no entry" no-
tices in their conversations? It is surely fear.

At the root of all of us, our inheritance from Adam, is a fear of taking root in the not-I, of being not only used by other people but even known by them. It is a fear lest the independence of our person be destroyed, for being open to other people in love means taking a risk, the risk of being involved and dependent upon others, the risk of exposure to other people's love. There is an instinct in us, inarticulate for the most part, which holds us back from breaking out of the security of our privacy and running this risk of being involved. This instinct tells us to remain in that security of privacy where there is no danger of being hurt or used by a fellow man, who by definition is out of our control. Another person as an intimate may make a number of demands upon us and upset the pattern of our lives in unpredictable ways. And so we elect sometimes not to love, choosing safety and quiet before danger and trouble. "I think I have always liked my fellow men. Liking is a great deal safer than love. It demands no victims," says Dr. Colin in Graham Greene's *A Burnt Out Case*. With fear we can handle likes and dislikes. Only love gets out of control. We do not readily offer ourselves as victims.

The tragedy is that modern city life produces an increasing number of people who shy away from the idea of being such victims. In the villages of a former age and the slum tenements of the last generation, privacy was impossible. Not surprisingly these milieux produced rich personalities. But the housing schemes and garden suburbia of the 1960's and 70's are built for privacy and fear. Behind the bright curtains and the multi-colored doors of the housing estate council houses and the tower blocks are many stunted persons, depriving themselves of the richest of human experiences. It is the characteristic problem of our age: the problem of mutual love and trust, of communication between individuals, who are thrown together as never before in our cities, but remain isolated within themselves. It is true that one cannot simply promote universal I-Thou relationships as the panacea for all ills because, as Harvey Cox pointed out, modern city living needs the superficial I-You relationship between uninvolved individuals if it is going to work at all. I cannot, in other words, be trying to get involved in every person in that train compartment! The easy taking up and putting down of superficial relationships is an obvious need in modern life. But when that is said, there is still the central need for all men to have persons in their lives whom they can love and be loved by, and the modern dilemma is to enable that to happen and promote its growth in the most discouraging atmosphere for such relationships that we have ever known.

It is not difficult to see the connection between these psychological and sociological ideas and the gospel of Jesus Christ. Jesus made the notion of entering into relations with other people, of loving others, central to his teaching. The enormous energy generated by his teaching (which was crowned by his life and death "for his brethren") was an energy of love. The apostles went out to *love* the world and teach all men that they could and must make the effort to love other men. We know that the initial mission was successful by the fact that we teach and try to practice the christian message today. In those days, as now, it answered the deepest need of man, that need to have his fears conquered and to love and be loved. The strength of the christian message lies in the fact that it makes that idea central. To begin with, it offers an explanation of why men have those deep-down fears which seem paradoxically to operate against what they most want!

The doctrine of original sin offers a mythical explanation of the origin of this alienation at the heart of man's dealings with God and men. There was an original act of separation from God which all later men have "inherited," and one of the first results of this inherited separation between man and God was to produce a division among men themselves. They built the Tower of Babel and were scattered abroad to the corners of the world, speaking different languages and unable any longer to communicate with each other. "I'm sorry, you and I don't speak the same language" is to this day one of the most wounding things that can be said to anyone who is trying to communicate with people. This inheritance of Babel is the most widespread and common factor on both the international and family scenes today.

The disciples of Jesus Christ presented his teachings as the answer to this predicament of man. The command now was to love all men. Jesus fixed no limit to the area of loving for his followers. The New Testament worked out that this meant a completely universal love. For us, it means that we have to love across a number of gaps which at first

33

sight we would not be inclined to try to cross with love, which we would in fact consider as impossible to cross. Such gaps as the temperament gap between individuals who are completely antipathetic to each other; or the creed gap between opposing religions; or the class gap which is so powerful because it is so easily accepted (Is *everybody* in the bus my equal?); or the color and race gap, which throws up barriers of apartheid — projections of that deep-seated desire to remain in a controllable situation, and not be exposed to strangers; or the age gap which makes parents and children speak a different language. This last gap is a good example of the difficulty involved in taking Jesus' teaching on love seriously. It means trying to sympathize with a generation which sees everything in a different light to oneself and which just "doesn't begin to understand" even the premises of one's own principles of living. This last gap is an "ideology gap," which is perhaps the most difficult to cross with love and sympathy, because it requires an effort of transposition of thought, of trying to understand a way of thinking which differs from one's own. Love is more difficult if mutually accepted thought patterns are absent. The post-conciliar Catholic Church demonstrates the problem involved in trying to maintain love across an ideology gap, as we see old and young, clergy and laity, struggling to love each other and stay within the one community of love while there are at least two widely differing understandings of what it means to be a christian and what the Church is. The tensions are so great that it is tempting to give up the attempt as a failure from the start. And yet christianity is only in the world because it made this "impossible commandment" the crucial one, in fact the only one that mattered.

The New Testament presented Jesus Christ as the Redeemer of man from this inheritance of fear and misunderstanding. He came, St. John said, to "gather together in unity the scattered children of God" (Jn. 11:52). His mission was to reverse the direction of sin, to "debabelize" mankind and bring them together in love and understanding in one spiritual family. There was a clear recognition that this was impossible for man alone and unaided, and that the Holy Spirit, God himself, had been sent to the followers of Jesus to weld them together and inspire them to unite all men. This Holy Spirit was the spirit of unity. He was thus the Spirit of Love who from the depths of each baptized christian's soul inspired him to be a man of love by casting out the fear which prevents love (1 John 4:18). Much of the teaching of the New Testament was worked out against the background of the first big dispute among the early christians which threatened to disrupt the newly acquired unity. This was the dispute about subjecting the gentile christian converts to the demands of the old Jewish law. Reading St. Paul's epistles one can catch the urgency of the debate and the danger felt that even after the Redemption of mankind from sin, men were going to fall into the old ways of disruption and misunderstanding. So there was a special urgency in the apostles who preached that *only* in Christ could unity be maintained, just as it was only in him that it had been achieved. There is, for instance, the teaching of the Epistle to the Ephesians about unity in Christ. The danger of disruption produced an eloquent answer setting forth the conditions on which unity among christians could be kept. "But now in Christ Jesus, you that used to be so far apart from us have been brought very close, by the blood of Christ. For he is the peace between us, and has made the two into one and broken down the barrier which used to keep them apart, actually destroying in his own person the hostility caused by the rules and decrees of the Law. This was to create one single New Man in himself out of the two of them and by restoring peace through the cross, to unite them both in a single Body and reconcile them with God. In his own person he killed the hostility" (Eph. 2: 13-16). And so christians saw that love was only possible for them if the Risen Christ himself was the principle of their loving. In him they could do all things, even say yes to their most difficult neighbors. Without him they could do nothing. "Dear Lord, you never tell us to do what is impossible, and yet you can see more clearly than I do how weak and imperfect I am; if, then, you tell me to love my sisters as you love them, that must mean that you yourself go on loving them in and through me — you know it couldn't be possible in any other way," said St. Thérèse of Lisieux echoing the same teaching years later (Autobiography of a Saint, p. 209). Thérèse is a good example of someone who had more than her share of native inhibitions and fears which made it difficult for her to break out of the security of her family and love other people. She found the courage to do so in her love for Jesus Christ which she then translated into love of her brethren. In the process she "made" her personality, and she who could well have been an unattractive, limited girl became one of the best-known and loved personalities of our times. In her courageously lived christianity she manifested the power of Christ to transform his disciples, whatever the natural material and however seemingly difficult it is for them to love.

The New Testament, however, does not look merely to Jesus Christ for the solution to man's problems of loving. It encourages us to look through Christ to the Godhead. Christ made his central moral exhortation to men that they must love. In doing this he was revealing the nature of man to men and behind that the nature of God to men. Jesus' importance was not only what he was in himself, perfect Man, but that he was the Word of God too, an explanation of God to men. We have seen that it was because man is what he is that he must love. Now we can reflect that this deep-seated need in man to communicate and break out of the prison of his fears is there because man is made in the image of God. This pattern of communicating was the essential pattern of the Godhead, before it became the essential pattern of manhood. For God is not Pure Being, existing in static solitude, as a too-Greek-inspired theology might suggest. He is, in the revelation of Jesus, Love as well as Being, a community of Persons, Father, Son and Holy Spirit, eternally existing in a dialogue of love, and communicating it to man. The God revealed to us by Christ is not static but dynamic, and the dynamism is one of love, of that self realization by going out to others which this chapter has been examining. It is all there in the Godhead before it was placed in man, God's creation. So the value of Jesus' revelation is that it gives a divine explanation of man's desire to lose himself in love and makes sense of our deep-seated urges. They are divine urges precisely because they exist in the Trinity before they exist in us. Behind the Incarnation, therefore, is the Holy Trinity, God in dialogue with himself, knowing and loving, Father, Son and Spirit. Meditating on this, St. John writes in his epistle that God *is* love. There could not be a simpler definition. It means for us that the "impossible commandment" is part of the fiber of humanity, which is created in the image and likeness of a trinitarian God. God is himself a system of personal communication; open, not shut; inviting, not repelling; including, not excluding; giving, not taking; in a word, loving. The impossible commandment; then, is not so impossible after all, if we consider that it answers a call in man placed there in imitation of God. The unnatural thing is not to love. We know that we can act unnaturally at times, but it is a comfort to know that our acts of sin and lack of loving are not part of our truest nature. They are only aberrations due to sin from which Jesus liberates us with his new life of grace, thus enabling us to become authentic children of the Father, fulfilling our true nature by being as like him as possible.

CHAPTER THREE

The Social
Commitment

In 1899 the scottish labor leader Keir Hardie
took issue against a prominent Glasgow industrialist of his day who was an upright
christian leading a devout family life, an eld-
er of his kirk and a noted philanthropist who
gave away £10,000 a year in charity. He was
well known on the Glasgow Town Council
for his stand for christian principles and
achieved a notable success when he pre-
vented the trams in the city running on Sun-
days. Keir Hardie took issue against this man
because workers in the Shawfield Chemical
Works, which he owned, were forced to
work twelve hours a day, seven days a week,
and were docked their Monday wages if they
missed work on Sunday. Keir Hardie pointed
out that while Lord Overtoun, the owner of

the chemical works, gave away 22/10d an hour every year in philanthropic charity, his workers only received 4d an hour for their labors. Seventy years later we begin to see the grotesque anomaly in such a life as Lord Overtoun's, but it has to be admitted that a social conscience is a comparatively recent restoration among christians. The nineteenth century abounds with examples of christian industrialists who led devout family lives (and often endowed their local churches) while grinding the faces of the poor in England's dark satanic mills. Much of that living by two standards has now disappeared from our society but we should not be too confident that this double christian think is no longer a danger for us. The generous lady in South America, owner of a string of race horses, who built new stables for her horses and kindly turned the old stables into houses for the poor, getting a cardinal along to bless these new dwellings, was convinced that she was performing an act of considerable charity beyond what was really expected of her by the Church. Nor need we go outside our own country for evidence that passive acceptance of sub-christian standards of society by christians who would describe themselves as fully practising is widespread. Such christians have been taught to lead fully committed private lives of personal charity and spirituality and think that to go further than that is an unnecessary mixing of religion and politics. Perhaps especially public school christianity, with its emphasis on loyalty to the status quo has tended to produce this mentality, at least up to the recent past. We are now busy catching up with a broadened christian outlook in our education and social living and, as so often, much of the running has been made for us by non-christian thinkers and activists in this field whose insights and work for social justice have been gladly taken over and baptized by committed christians. Although it is true, we Catholics should not, perhaps, be too loud in our proclamation to the world that work for social justice is an original christian activity, considering that we have largely learned it in the present day from agnostics and "enemies of the Church."

The fact is that the call to follow Christ in person-to-person love, with all the effort required to overcome our native reluctance as we outlined in the previous chapter, has always been seen by christians as central to their discipleship of Christ and, though we have frequently failed in this, we have never lost the vision of its necessity. Saying yes to our neighbor has always been regarded as a first duty of christians. But saying yes to society, being personally concerned about the way the society one lives in is conducted, has tended to be a Cinderella among the christian virtues. While micro-ethics have loomed large in the thoughts of christians, macro-ethics have sometimes been completely forgotten. This chapter is about the latter because it is no longer possible to postpone consideration of this problem which is clearly going to be the major one for the future of christian love in the world. However alien it may be to our background and tradition, we have to face the problems posed by political christianity and cannot sweep them out of sight by ignorance or unconcern.

Two historical facts help to focus this problem for us today. The first is that the Catholics of this country have a history which makes it hard for them to think in terms of co-responsibility within society. The great majority of Catholics in England, Scotland and Wales are the descendants of Irish immigrants. Some have been in this country for a number of generations, while a significant proportion are first generation immigrants. Both kinds live within a strong racial tradition of exclusion from and and non-cooperation with the government of society. For generations Irish Catholics have been "émigrés de l'intérieure," living geographically in the country but not thinking of themselves as fully accepted members of the country and not in fact wanting much to be so. That is now, of course, a dying tradition but traditions die slowly and leave unconscious traces long after they have been consciously rejected. Few young Catholics today would consider themselves as alien to the country they have been brought up in, but traces of the past can still be found, chiefly in this very matter of not being too fussy about sub-christian standards in public life and politics in general, since they are not thought of as matters which the individual citizen ought to do anything about. A great number of the Catholics who leave our schools have imbibed a personal, private attitude to salvation which has a long way to go before it can properly be called communal. The second historical fact is the wider one that even outside christianity the idea that all persons in the state are meant to play an active part and have a say in the way it is run is in practice comparatively strange, however much it has been accepted in theory before. The Long Revolution from 1789 to this day has been long because it has been slow and only today, as Raymond Williams points out, are we beginning to think of everybody's relationship to the state in terms of being a "member" of the community instead of "subject" or "servant" with only a passive interest in matters of state.

As well as being personal, salvation is also socio-political. By this is meant not so much that religion has to do with what goes on in the House of Commons or Congress as that it is concerned necessarily with the public standards of society as well as the private standards of the individual. This may well cause some christians to take to a life of active politics in paliament, but what it chiefly implies is that everyone should be conscientiously concerned about the running of society. Man is social by nature; he develops by relating to other people. We saw this in the previous chapter. But this very fact means that as well as being concerned about his personal relationships and seeing that they are conducted in the spirit of Christ, the christian must be equally concerned that society itself be christian. We do not only work and pray that our adjustment to other people be as christian as possible, but also we have to work to see that society itself is adjusted to the mind of Christ. The christian industrialist is not doing enough as a follower of Christ if he is merely being privately loving in his personal relationships. His main concern has to be that his industry is conducted along christian lines, justice and love being the laws by which it operates, not merely economic rules. The failure to do this in the past was the scandal of victorian christianity. The christian philanthropists who gave away large sums to good causes were not philanthropists at all when those sums were made by unjust means or when fellow men and women suffered in order to increase their riches. A change of heart is needed for everyone who accepts Christ as Lord, but it is a change of heart which must lead to effective action to christianize and maintain as christian any society in which one has influence. If this metanoia stays within the private life of the individual it is not fully christian. We have to be concerned wtih christianizing the structures of the society we live in if our attempts to be christian are to have any validity before God or meaning before men in the secular city of today. This is a high task and we should not have any illusions about its difficulty. For if there exist obstacles within us to establishing loving relations with our neighbor in our private lives, there are equally deep-rooted obstacles which make us slow to bring our christian principles into public, communal life. We so easily talk about not mixing religion and politics or about leading quietly christian lives and not interfering with other people. It is not difficult to see that these are versions of the radical refusal to become involved in others, this time in the public conduct of society rather than private personal relations. The man who "doesn't want to interfere" conveniently forgets that merely by endorsing a status quo and by trading in society he is already interfering according to a certain way. The question he has to ask is whether his involvement in society is christian as it stands and whether he is going to do anything about it if he finds that it is not. In other words he has to become as aware of the hidden macro-ethical dimensions of his life as the micro-ethical dimensions of which he is probably keenly aware.

Radical christians go further and say that the political, structurally orientated commitment of the christian is the primary commitment of the follower of Christ, while the person-to-person relationship to his neighbor only has meaning within the former concern. They point out that the society a man lives in is important to his formation and growing more so every day in our technological civilization. It is quite simply not possible to regard man in society today as a unit without taking into account the society he lives in, and the main ethical concern of any intelligent observer must be about the social forces at work round about the individual. Modern christians are rightly suspicious of a spirituality which leave out the social dimension and concerns itself only with personal prayer and exercises of piety. Prayer and piety must center around the communal christian response if they are to have any validity in modern society. This means that piety will issue forth in attempts to do something about conditions in society, not in attempts to adjust people to living within existing situations which are not just. Christ came to liberate men from slavery, not merely to ameliorate their lot within it. Christians who spend their time ameliorating rather than liberating are only partially answering the demands of Christ upon them and rightly earning the criticism that religion for them is opium to lull people, whereas for Jesus Christ it was leaven to stir people up. Christianity should fill us with a "divine discontent" not only about our personal inadequacies before God and men but about the community inadequacy of racial, social, economic injustice which surrounds us all in the twentieth century.

So far in this chapter we have spoken about the community we live in without adverting to what exactly is meant by that. In modern conditions the community we live in is in fact the entire world. Communications have made the world shrink to the size of a village. This is no exaggeration. We can sit in our own homes every night and not only read about events all over the world but even see them happening before our eyes on television. We know as much about far-off countries and the events in them as former generations knew about events in the next-door town. The result is that it is not really possible to ignore what is happening to our fellow men at the other end of the world, however much their troubles may be spacially remote from us. This very fact, however, brings with it an enormous difficulty. Communications have made it possible for our *knowledge* to be worldwide. But our ability to take effective action about what we see is no greater than it was before and perhaps less, as society becomes more technically complex. Thus we are in a different situation from mediaeval man. He could not only find out about what was happening at the other end of his village but he could also do something effective about it. The outreach of his knowledge and his ability to act were equal. It is not so with us. We can know what is happening in our "village" but we can do very little about it. The only thing most citizens can do is make a protest, which though it is not direct action is an attempt to get others to take direct action. In our large democracies it may not be very effective action, but it is at least action. This is surely why protest has become an important element in society today. It is a reflection of the growing social conscience among ordinary people as they react to the news they read and see in the news media. Like all christian activities it is open to abuses, but in itself it is surely a truly christian way of saying yes to social commitments. Just because our society has expanded to include Russia, China, U.S.A., Asia, Africa, South America, India, Malaysia as well as Great Britain and Europe, First, Second and Third Worlds alike, we have to be aware of what is going on in those places and form a christian conscience about the news we receive.

A second reason why protest is part of the christian response is one that has not always been remembered in the past, namely that there is in christianity a built-in element of unrest vis à vis the status quo. Jesus himself inherited the tradition of the Jewish prophets of making a protest against the leaders of society if they manifested a tendency to become corrupt. The christianity which he founded began as a movement of dissociation from the established respectable religion of its day. This is not to deny that christianity is among other things institutional, but merely to point out that the institutional element needs constantly to be balanced by the more antiseptic element of protest, in order to purify the sources of action in Church and world. We know that all power tends to corrupt, and therefore it is part of the christian responsibility to watch lest leaders in Church and state slide into this corruption. Once again, it is not sufficient to lead decent private christian lives without thought or concern for the communal issues. Following Christ has never been meant to be a quiet or easy affair, and there has to be always this uneasy element of criticism in the Church "rocking the boat" to prevent the revolutionary gospel of Jesus imperceptibly becoming a movement merely to keep the peaceful status quo going. The prophet Micah summed up his message: "This is what Yahweh asks of you: only this, to act justly, to love tenderly, and to walk humbly with your God" (Micah 6:8). In the past, christians have tended to try to love tenderly and walk humbly with God more energetically than they have tried to act justly in Church and state. Finally, it should not be thought that protesting is easy, for the man who protests has to remember that, like the power against which he is making his demonstration, protest also tends to corrupt, and the need to keep in mind Jesus' words about motes and beams is never more needed than by the christian when he is being urged to make a protest. Unless he examines himself and listens to the criticisms of others he risks falling away from christianity himself. We can all too easily pass from being a Palm Sunday crowd to a Good Friday mob without reflection.

It is important to keep together the two dimensions of charity, the personal and the social. This is not easy, because there is in most men a native bias towards either one or the other. We are either, by our psychological make-up, person-centered or system-centered. But following Christ is meant to be an integrating force in our lives, so we have to cultivate, under the inspiration of the Holy Spirit, the particular development which we find difficult. Those who are basically liberal and personalist in their approach to human problems have to develop an interest in the social problems of the community, and those who are naturally radical and community-centered have to deepen their approach to life so that it allows room for the personal values of friendship and love without which all concern about society is a waste of time. In Arnold Wesker's *Chicken Soup with Barley*, Sarah Kahn, the political activist, ends by revealing that what made her political was love for people, not ideas. "You'll die, you'll die — if you don't care you'll die. Ronnie, if you don't care, you'll die," is her last cry to her uncaring son.

The way to keep both branches of christian love together is to surrender to both equally generously, and it is the practice of this, rather than any theorizing, that maintains the proper development. In practice, the christian who wants to enforce the person-to-person love taught by Jesus finds himself face to face with the social issue. Charity to this neighbor who is a colored immigrant or that priest who is having a disagreement with his bishop about *Humanae Vitae* involves the political issue from the start, and one cannot escape from the political question without also escaping from charity. Try as some of us may to live the apolitical life of "pure charity," we cannot succeed. Love forces us to take sides. Commitment to Christ does not take place in a platonic sphere outside the politics of the here and now. It takes place in the world about us with its live issues, both big and small, or it is not commitment at all. In other words, immediately we try to love people across the gaps and barriers in society today, we find that love has to do something about removing those gaps and barriers, or it is not really love. Love begins by loving across the creed, class, color gaps but to survive as love at all it has to do its best to abolish those senseless barriers in our society. It abolishes them most effectively, of course, by making its political activity an intensely loving act. Again, if we start at the other end by considering the christian desire to take political action, we find that the complementary branch of person-to-person love is involved as well. Those who have taken part in a christian demonstration find that the common activity for a social end generates a very real person-to-person love among the demonstrators and, eventually, this love extends to those outside the demonstration as well, and even finally to the police who are controlling it. This should not surprise us when we consider that Christ is present in all such gatherings. His love cannot be compartmentalized into the personal and social pigeon-holes of human theories, but is one and undivided. It is both political and personal at once. In fact the absence of personal love and the presence of backbiting and hate among political activists is the best sign that theirs is not a christian movement, however impressive its claims on paper.

The life of Jesus Christ manifested this integration of all the elements in loving. He was both a personalist caring about human relationships and a revolutionary upsetting the status quo. It is not possible to tie him down to either one or the other. Both elements were present in his apostolate and each fertilized the other. On the one hand there is no doubt about his teaching about charity. It is to be found on nearly every page of the gospel insisting unequivocally on universal love for all people whatever the social relationship between lover and loved, and clearly this was practised by him as he attracted so many widely different characters to himself. On the other hand he cannot be stereotyped as a kind and gentle man who gave no offence to anyone, because he manifestly did give offence to the rulers of the Jewish Establishment and did so on purpose. In the midst of his teaching on personal charity there was his political apostolate to break down the narrow nationalistic barriers of the Law which involved direct conflict with the rules of the Jews. Jesus was not persecuted for his teaching on neighborly love until it became clear that by this he meant to break through the barriers of the Law and so threaten the position of the rulers of the Jewish religion. It was a case of love beginning to abolish the barriers it found in society, of love having to be political as well as personalist. Perhaps Jesus' attitude to charity is best seen in his parable of the Good Samaritan, which was his answer to the question "Who is my neighbor?" The story is a story of personal love and involvement, but it contained within it a social challenge by making the politically acceptable priest and the levite fail to act as neighbors to the man in need of help, and the politically unacceptable samaritan do so. It was a lesson in personal love with an unmistakable political purpose. Jesus Christ did not draw back from either implication, and left his followers to face the same integrated challenge through the ages.

CHAPTER FOUR

Prayer is a Sign of Life

If the whole of life with its personal and social commitments is prayer, is there any need for the specific activity we call praying? That is the question asked by a great number of christians in this decade. Doubtless it is a question that has always concerned christians, but it is particularly relevant today as christians all over the world wake up from a kind of sleep of "spirituality" and begin to take their task of actively renewing the face of the earth seriously. If this active task of "saying yes" to God in the renewal of society today is itself prayer, as we have outlined in the first three chapters, what is the status of the distinct act of praying on one's knees? Is it a waste of time or is it still relevant?

One answer to that question is given by the Dutch Catechism which warns that a life lived without any distinct act of prayer runs the risk of ceasing to be over-all prayerful.

> "At the most difficult moment of his life
> Jesus gave the warning: 'Watch and pray
> that you may not enter into temptation;
> the spirit indeed is willing but the flesh is
> weak' (Matt. 26:41). We cannot do with-
> out watchfulness. Otherwise obedience
> will deteriorate into self-will. The sense
> of the presence of God will vanish, and
> at the moment of trial we will forget his
> will and disregard it. There can be no
> work without contemplation, no expan-
> sion without exploration in depth. Love
> cannot exist without self-expression"
> (Pp. 311-312).

All this is very true, and we have the example of Jesus himself to convince us that prayer is a worthwhile operation. After days of
complete self-giving to his neighbors Jesus
would go apart and spend nights in prayer
and, as the Catechism noted, he preceded
his supreme act of redemption by spending
hours of prayer in Gethsemane. He would
not have indulged in this practice of prayer
if it was irrelevant or against the rest of his
teaching. Still less would he have taught his
disciples to pray. Precisely because he did
pray and taught others to pray, we are en-

titled to go deeper into this matter and look for reasons why prayer as a specific activity is not irrelevant but worthwhile both for Jesus and ourselves.

Prayer is a verbalization, an articulation, of the implicit yes to God which is the christian life. We have seen in the previous chapters that christian living is saying yes through all the events of life, yes to people and yes to society, and that this yes is ultimately and most intimately uttered to the Father. That is what the fruit of grace is: the Spirit-inspired ability to speak to God in Christ as Father, to say "Abba." We utter this abba when we live our christian lives generously among people. But this love, this relationship to the Father through the events of life, needs to be made explicit. That is the way love works. It does not stop short at a merely implicit relationship to the Beloved but goes further to articulate and make explicit the implicit yes of the partnership. Christian prayer is thus a moment of focus for the whole of christian life, a moment when we make explicit the implicit direction of our lives. Our whole lives are saying yes to God, in people and society, but we need to make this evident, to say it directly to our Father. When we stay still for a moment and pray, we turn directly to God and give him our whole lives. Thus prayer is not an operation in the gaps of life which we have to stop living to perform, or turn aside from our commmitments to do so. It is the focussing of our attention upon God so that we can give ourselves, commitments and all, to him more meaningfully. We never live more fully as christians than when we turn the whole direction of our lives towards God and give them totally to him. Doing this is not escaping from life into a side issue but charging our life with renewed energy and zeal. It is the central act of that faith, hope and charity which grace enables us to live. By saying yes to God explicitly in prayer we ensure that the life from the center of which this cry has gone up is itself a steady yes to people and society and through them to God. Without those explicit moments of prayer there is a real danger that the lives of christians in this world may be only theoretically lived as prayer. In practice you can only pray all the time everywhere if you bother to pray some of the time somewhere.

A good way of explaining this is to say that prayer for the christian is a generative sign of his life. It is worthwhile to examine that phrase. Prayer is first a sign of christian living, that is, a gesture which sums up, demonstrates, what that living is all about. On our knees in prayer before God we make ourselves into a sign, a demonstration to Him, of what we want the whole of our life to be. Prayer *signifies* that the rest of our living is also worship of the Father. It bears the relationship to what we do before and after we pray of being a sign. It is therefore not an interlude in living which has no relevance to what goes before and comes after it. On the contrary it is a zone of intensity, which has the fullest possible meaning for the rest of life. It is a pregnant gesture. Our day-to-day lives are full of such signs and gestures which sum up what our living is about. A kiss or a handshake are signs of this kind. The whole of marriage is not kissing, but to kiss is to signify what marriage is about. Friends do not spend their time shaking hands together but when they do it is a gesture which "means" their friendship. To abolish kissing and shaking hands because they were not useful and did not get on with the business of living would be to miss the point about signs in daily living. We do not as a rule think out the theory of signs from day to day, but we would instinctively know the loss if they were taken from us. In the same way christians pray instinctively as a sign of their service of God in daily life and would feel the loss intensely if they were not allowed to do so. But prayer is not a bare sign of christian living, it is a *generative* sign. Prayer generates further intense christian living. It inspires what it is at the same time signifying. After praying the christian is more ready to serve God in life. The prayer has made him more prompt and worshipful towards the Lord. In other words, we pray in order to worship God more zealously in the whole of our lives. Hence in calling prayer a sign we must point out that it is a generative sign. The zone of intensity radiates power beyond itself. Here again this is true of the ordinary gestures of day-to-day life. The kiss exchanged by married couples unites them more closely as well as signifying their already achieved union. The handshake of friends not only shows that they are friends, it also *makes* them friends. In marriage intercourse between the partners is the supreme example of a sign of their love which generates further union, and it is the tradition of christianity to liken the act of prayer to that act. In the marriage between the christian soul and God, prayer acts as the supreme act of love which both signifies and generates the union. To neglect it on the grounds that it is irrelevant or an interruption in the business of making the whole of our life a prayer is clearly to miss the point about love.

We can get a deeper understanding of the place of prayer in christianity if we consider the way in which the doctrine of grace has been described in christian theology. In explaining this mystery, theology and revelation make it apparent that by grace man is enabled to relate personally to God so that his whole life is capable of becoming a personal relationship within the Trinity to the Father through the Son in the Spirit. Grace has been described as "a permanent disposition which capacitates man for an I-Thou relationship with God, and is manifested in the personal communication of faith, hope and charity" (Juan Alfaro). If this is so, it should be plain that grace enables a man to enter into the deepest possible kind of human relationship with God, one that is equal to and even surpasses the relationships he has with his fellow men. The love a man is enabled to have for God may indeed be dependent in this life on faith and conducted in hope and therefore at times be dim and bleak, but the Bible is sure that it is a deep and lasting union comparable to the other deep and lasting unions we have in this world, wife with husband, son with father, child with mother. In other words, grace enables us to *love* God. That being so, it does not do justice to the biblical and theological truth to regard the christian life as one merely of joint work and action with God. That is not how love is expressed by men; it leaves out the dimension of generative sign which is integral to human loving. Lovers *need* to express their love with a loving gesture, not just as a luxury for leisure moments but as the central act of their living and loving together. Thus in marriage the husband and wife spend their lives working for each other, but that mutual work and service is not the central part of their marriage. The central part is their enjoyment of each other's company, their intercourse together. The marriage where the wife was too busy looking after the needs of her husband to talk to him or give herself to him would not be a true love match. Sometimes one comes across such marriages and discovers that the frantic busyness of both spouses for each other's well-being is often an escape from a deeper meeting with each other which they are too scared to risk. The essence of the I-Thou relationship is the spending of time together, the *wasting* of time from a utilitarian point of view, for love is essentially daft. It is the same with the "graced" christian and God. Each wants the person of the other, not just a mutual service or joint participation in action. The tradition of many centuries of christianity has in fact borne this out, for in every age the deepest christian relationship has been seen to be that of prayer and there have been few saints who have not "wasted time" in hours of prayer.

The traditional way of speaking about the relationship between prayer and life has been to talk about prayer first and then show how it overflows into life. In this book we have been doing the opposite; we have begun with the christian attitude to living and proceeded from there to speak about prayer as the generative sign of that christian attitude, the explicit yes which articulates the implicit yes. We have done this not because we think it wrong to start with prayer — there is a long christian tradition which speaks of the spiritual life as the bringing to others of the fruits of contemplation. But many today find it less satisfactory to make the start with prayer and prefer to start at the other end with concrete christian living. This is not the place to go into the historical reasons why moderns prefer to start at this end but it is clear that they do; the empirical inductive method is about the only one which brings satisfaction to modern scientific men. That is why we have introduced prayer as the sign which makes sense of already attempted christian living rather than as a necessary preliminary to such living. The success of the books by Michael Quoist and his imitators which begin with ordinary "non-spiritual" things like five-pound notes, helping down-and-outs, being jilted in love, shows that the approach to prayer through the problems of life is the most satisfactory one for modern people. We are, perhaps with justification, suspicious today of an approach which does not plunge us straightaway into the hurlyburly of ordinary living. Not to do this carries with it a suggestion of being out of touch and in an ivory tower, and christians are rightly sensitive about that charge in the present age. There is always going to be a need for contemplation in the christian life but, as Dag Hammarskjold said, "In our era, the road to holiness necessarily passes through the world of action." Dag Hammarskjold also coined the phrase about life being a journey inward. Perhaps best of all that sums up the modern approach to prayer. It is not so much a journey from the inside

outward, a passage from the interior life to
the exterior, but a journey from the outside
inwards, a discovery in depth of the springs
of outward action. We have to start at the
outside, at the busy mess and muddle of
modern living where we try to say yes to the
Father from the situation of factory, office
and housing area. Starting from there, where
Christ is alongside us in the modern world,
we travel inwards to find Christ again, this
time at the center of our beings, at the still
point which makes sense of the turning
world. Linking up those two presences of
Christ is the whole adventure of prayer today, and it works best when we start with
the Christ in life all around us and penetrate
to the Christ in our hearts rather than vice
versa.

People are sometimes puzzled by the
place of Christ in modern prayer. Is he out
there, the divine Leader, who is our Saviour
and to whom we address our petitions, or is
he in some mysterious way present within
us inspiring us to lead Christ-like lives in
the world? Catholics especially, who were
brought up on the easily understood devotions to the Sacred Heart, Precious Blood,
Good Shepherd, can become very muddled
by the frequent references to the Christ of

the Secular City or to the Negro Christ which are heard nowadays. They can become bewildered by the apparently endless "presences" of Christ in the modern world which are made much of in religious-minded journalism. There is, however, little cause for muddle if it is remembered that the Risen Christ, God and man at the same time, does indeed have many presences in the world, but that there are two basic ways in which the christian can think of him. First of all we can think of Christ as the object of our worship and admiration. This is the way many older catholics were brought up to think of Christ. He is the term and goal of devotion. We imitate him in our lives and pray to him in our prayers. Out of this form of christo-centricism came the many devotions which center on Christ as object, like the Stations of the Cross, devotion to the Sacred Heart, meditation on the historical life of Jesus, and especially Benediction and Exposition of the Blessed Sacrament. The governing factor in all these ways of approaching Christ is the consciousness of him as term and object of christian devotion. If this, however, were the only way of thinking of the Risen Christ it would be a true but jejune understanding of the New Testament. Fortunately the way in

70

which St. Paul thought of Christ is wide-spread in the Church today. For St. Paul, Christ was a real person indeed, but he did not think of him as the object and term of our devotions. Rather, Christ was the subject of our christian life, the Living Principle in which christians live the new life of grace. The phrase "in Christ" occurs frequently in St. Paul's epistles, and by it he tries to show how the christian lives a new life with Christ as *subject*. The christian approaches the Father in Christ, worships and adores in Christ, loves his neighbors in Christ, in fact does all things "whatsoever" in this Risen Christ. In this way of understanding, the object and term of christian devotion is the Father, not Christ. The latter is the principle in whom we dare to approach the Father because only in him can we do so. In other words this is christocentricism but in a subjective, not objective, sense. It is christocentric with regard to the inner inspiration of our worship, but insofar as the goal of devotions is concerned it is Father-centered. This is the way the Liturgy looks at Christ, for the Liturgy does not normally address prayers to Christ, but prays to the Father *through* Christ. The Mass, not Benediction or Exposition, is the central act of this form of christianity, and the Doxology at the end of the Canon in which priest and people unite to give all honor and glory to the Father through, with and in the Son, is the supreme expression of this more biblical way of thinking. Realization of the subjective presence of Christ in us all (rather than his objective presence "out there") gives rise, of course, to all those "presences" of Christ in the Negro, the Down-and-Out, the Starving, which modern consciousness is increasingly taking seriously. We should not find this bewildering if we reflect that Christ is genuinely present in all his brothers, and that the principle of unity for this universal brotherhood is the one Father who is the uniting factor and term of reference for a varied world.

If we understand what subjective christocentricism means it becomes clear how prayer today can be described as a journey from the Christ who is to be found in the world around us, especially in the people we meet, towards the Christ who has to be discovered and continually rediscovered in the depths of our being. If we add that Christ is also the principle in whom we are enabled to say the various yeses which make up the truly christian response, we can begin to see how our lives are bathed in the presence of Christ and how true it is that without him we can do nothing, least of all make valid prayer to the Father.

CHAPTER FIVE

Creation, Incarnation and Secularization

One of the most helpful notions in understanding the true nature of Creation and Incarnation is the modern one of "man come of age." As this is a phrase which arouses both fears and enthusiasms, it is worth examining in some detail in order to deepen our knowledge of the way God works in the world and thus our understanding of the place of prayer.

All men, when faced with the world about them, can distinguish an area which is open to their understanding and under their control. The rest is an area which is not understood by them and is outside their control. These areas have been labelled the secular and the sacred, because the first area, under man's dominion, is plainly one which "belongs" to life in this world, while the area outside man's knowledge and control is mysterious by definition, the area inhabited by the gods. Man lives his life partly in the secular and partly in the sacred. For primitive man the area of the secular, under his control, was very small, while the area of the mysterious and sacred was vast — his knowledge of this world was extremely limited. For instance, the area of understanding in the curing of diseases was small, which left the area of the mysterious very big. Since not many cures based on science were known, most of the cures were effected by having recourse to sacred influences, the witch doctor. This was the function of religion: to effect "business" in the area which was outside man's control, by prayer and sacrifice. Because of the hugeness of this area for primitive man, religion played a very big part in his life. For instance, religious sacrifices for a good harvest or successful hunting were more important than an approach to these problems based on science, which scarcely existed.

It is not hard to see how the balance between the secular and the sacred, understood as above, has changed enormously in the modern world. Modern scientific man has pushed the area of the known secular out to the limits, leaving the area of the unknown sacred very small indeed. We know so much more about medicine and crops; our area of knowledge is enormous compared to that of primitive man. In fact, in principle, the area of the secular has been pushed out to the extreme limits, leaving nothing for the sacred and mysterious. For instance, although cancer is still a problem which man has not solved and therefore in fact still belongs to the mysterious, man knows that research could one day conquer this problem; so in principle cancer belongs to the area of the controllable secular. Modern man has, therefore, done away with the necessity of having recourse to the gods as a substitute for doing something himself. Religion in that sense is no longer needed and modern man can therefore be described as "religionless." He no longer bows before the mystery of the universe and its unknown workings, but goes on researching till he discovers its secrets. This can aptly be called coming of age. Children are powerless in the face of scientific mysteries, but adults set about discovering their secrets. In this sense it is right to describe man today as come of age.

THE CHRISTIAN AFFIRMATION

The reaction of scientific humanists to the realization that Religion was no longer needed by man in his search for knowledge and control of the universe was understandably a movement towards agnosticism if not atheism. This in turn produced a certain panic among christians who accepted the definitions of religion and sacred given above. But the reaction of more thinking christians was to reflect upon the meaning of the christian revelation concerning Creation and Incarnation and point out that the discoveries of modern science did not threaten but supported the true christian view given in the Bible. The fallacy in the above definitions of secular and sacred when applied to christianity lies in the separation of secular and sacred into areas which did not overlap. It is true that for primitive man and, perhaps all non-christian religions, the area governed by the power of the gods and that governed by man's knowledge were mutually exclusive; religion took over where science gave way. But in the christian scheme of things this is the opposite of the truth. Creation, in the Bible, was a kind of sharing; man was made in the image and likeness of God and was placed over the universe as God's vice-gerent. This meant that man began to play

God's role in the universe, but God did not cease to inhabit the world; his Presence remained everywhere and most especially was in man who was doing his work in the world. In other words, in the christian understanding of Creation man and God are not rivals with God only acting where man does not, but they are partners, with God working everywhere in the world but most especially in and through man. The christian God, therefore, is not a "deus ex machina" who comes to the rescue of man at the point when he can no longer know and control the world, a god to be placated by religious sacrifice when human knowledge has broken down. The true God is one who is always and everywhere present and who works most effectively through man, who is the creature most like him in the universe. For the Bible the sacred is coterminous with the secular, being not a separate area of creation but a deeper dimension of the secular. God is not one more physical force at the limits of the world, but the undergirding metaphysical ground of all being, present and giving existence to every physical force. The more man seeks to understand and control the universe the more he is doing what God wants him to do. Man's scientific successes in this age are not, therefore, disasters which threaten the position of God in man's estimation, but are causes of great joy because they are the successes of God through man. An act of God is not necessarily, in the christian understanding, an act outside human control (as it is for insurance companies), but an act of any secondary cause in creation; this not only includes the acts of man but refers particularly to them since man is God's chief "actor" in creation.

The christian God does not only hold sway over the part of the physical universe we do not yet understand but will one day. Obviously a god like that belongs to the pre-scientific past and his days are numbered; *that* god is dying in the modern world. But Yahweh, the God of the Bible and the Father of Jesus Christ, is powerfully present everywhere in his creation, in the parts man has mastered as well as those he has not. He is to be found at the heart of the secular. This means that in christianity the sacred is not a separate area other than the world of science and everyday life, but is to be found in and through the secular. The sacred in christianity is a deeper dimension to the secular, not another part of life. Our approach to God, therefore, is not that of men who despair of their human efforts succeeding and so take to prayer as the final solution. We approach God at the beginning of every human enterprise and pray that he may help us to succeed, for our success will be his success. We do not resort to God when everything has gone wrong but go to him at times of success as well as failure. This was one of the insights of Dietrich von Bonhoeffer in prison in his letters to Eberhard Bethge:

"How wrong it is to use God as a stop-gap for the incompleteness of our knowledge. For the frontiers of knowledge are inevitably being pushed further and further, which means that you only think of God as a stop-gap. He is also being pushed back further and further, and is in more or less continuous retreat. We should find God in what we do know, not in what we don't; not in outstanding problems, but in those we have already solved.

"Religious people speak of God when human perception is (often just from laziness) at an end, or human resources fail; it is in fact always the Deus ex machina they call to their aid either for the so-called solving of insoluble problems or as support in human failure — always, that is to say, helping out human weakness or on the borders of human existence. . . .

81

It always seems to me that in talking thus we are only seeking frantically to make room for God. I should like to speak of God not on the borders of life but at its center, not in weakness but in strength, not therefore in man's suffering and death but in his life and prosperity."

In making these statements to his friends from prison, Bonhoeffer was overstating his case, for while it is right to emphasize that God is to be found in the strengths and successes of man it is not true to suggest that God is not to be found in man's weakness as well. God is to be found everywhere, and is often more obviously discovered when we fail than when we succeed. God's ways of working are traditionally most manifest when the best laid schemes of men go astray, so that the human instinct which looks for God at the end of the human tether is a theologically sound one, as long as it is remembered that God is at work before that too. Nevertheless, Bonhoeffer was making an important point when he insisted that God is to be looked for in the strengths and successes of man, for he was combatting a tendency in christianity to do nothing and leave all the work to God, the tendency almost to manufacture failure in order to rely on God more.

This is the quietistic tendency which likes to make religion an opium in the face of an all-powerful Fate, instead of a leaven for action. It panders to human laziness (as Bonhoeffer noticed above) and was a danger especially in protestant devotional practices because of the Reformation tendency to strengthen the position of grace at the expense of nature. To a Catholic, at least in theory, there is no extra need to emphasize the presence of God in the world, of grace in nature, for catholic theology has always insisted that grace works through nature and that secondary causes are autonomous in their own order and are instruments of, not rivals to, the First Cause. But the Reformation tendency was to promote the position of grace and demote the position of nature, as if the former demanded the latter. Bonhoeffer's insights help us to reverse that direction of thought by stressing the presence of grace in a strong nature as well as a weak one. As we have already said, the successes of the natural *are* the successes of the supernatural, for the latter has no ordinary way of working in the world other than through nature. Man comes of age because of God, not in spite of him.

All that we have said about Creation applies equally to Redemption. Here too, the notion of partnership, not of rivalry, is the truly biblical one. Christ redeemed mankind and the Church is the extended presence of the Redeeming Christ in the world today. But being redeemed by Christ does not mean that the baptized christian is absolved from further acts. On the contrary, the fact of being redeemed enables man to act with Christ in the world today. It is not a question of Christ taking over and working miracles when men in the Church have ceased. Christ works in the world today through the Church. Christianity is an active participation in Christ's activity among mankind, and Christ's activity is coterminous with the activity of christians. The signs of the kingdom in Jesus' day were the healing of the sick, the setting free of prisoners and the preaching of the gospel to the poor. These signs should be present in the world today by the activity of christians to that effect, for when christians do those things it is Christ doing them. Christ acts through his brothers, not apart from them. If we understood this properly we should understand that the works of Christ today are not only extraordinary acts of healing like the miracles of Lourdes, but also the ordinary human (i.e. christian) acts of healing through the hospitals and clinics of the health service. In the secular activity of christians (professed or anonymous) is to be discerned the sacred activity of the Risen Christ. The uncovenanted miracles of healing in the world are indeed marvelous signs of God's love, but there is a sense in which the "secular" acts of healing are more marvelous still, because they are evidence of the presence of the power of Christ in the ordinary works of this world, and are evidence that because of the Incarnation and Redemption this world has been saved. Secular acts of healing are sacred acts of healing as much as the miracles of Lourdes. The meaning of the biblical comparisons of Christ's working in his brethren to the Vine working in its branches or the Head working in the Body is precisely that. Our union with the Risen Christ means that all our acts are in principle sacred, not just some special ones with a religious label. As we said in the previous chapter, our lives are christocentric not because they center on Christ but because they are interiorly united to Christ here and now and in him we perform all our acts towards the world and the Father. We are bathed in the presence of Christ.

In this understanding of Creation and Redemption, has religious mystery disappeared entirely from the world? By no means. It has disappeared as the name we use for the physical forces in the world we have not yet mastered, but it reappears as the name we use for the heart of the secular which no one but God can understand. In saying that there are no mysteries left in principle for science we mean that there need not be any physical mysteries left if the search for scientific discovery continues. (Scientists are the first to say that this situation is a long way off.) But if there need not be any physical mysteries left in the world this is not to say that the whole scientifically mastered universe is not at a deeper level, the level of purpose and ultimate explanation, an eternal mystery known only to God. Instead of using the word mystery to describe scientific unknowns, it is better to use it for the area of ultimate purpose, because *this* area is the area of true religion. Here, at the heart of the secular and not in a separate world, is the true sacred, the truly mysterious. Here, therefore, adoration is due. Scientific discovery has not affected this area except possibly to make it more wonderful as we uncover the marvels of God's creation in human terms. Scientific discovery cannot affect this area, because it is an area which is not susceptible to empirical measurement. Science tries to answer the question "how?" and the more it succeeds the more marvellous God appears. Religion tries to answer the question "why?" or at least centers around that question, and finds the answer not in answers at all but in adoration.

Mystery is not absent from the modern world in spite of its progressive uncovering of scientific secrets, for the very unravelling of these scientific "mysteries" only serves to enhance the underlying incomprehensibility, mystery, that such a world should exist. This means that there is still very much a place for adoration in today's world. There is even a place for intercessory prayer. It has been suggested that intercession is no longer needed in the scientific age because it belongs to that age when it acted as an accompaniment to ignorance. Since we now study meteorology is there any need to pray for good weather? Since we study medicine is there any need to ward off plagues with prayers? The answer to these queries lies in the understanding of prayer as a generative sign which we discussed in the previous chapter. It is true that prayer is not a substitute for action and that it is a misuse of religion to use it as a rival activity to research and work. Prayer is not meant to be a substitute for action but its *sign*. When we pray we act out a gesture to signify that we are undertaking, under God's sovereignty and according to his will, to do our best to solve by all possible human means the problem before us. We think and hope that what we pray for is what God wants, and therefore these prayers are signs that we are ready to work for the good of God's kingdom in this world. Furthermore, our prayer not only signifies our intention to work but also generates the energy to do so. We rise from our knees more ready to start working or to continue the work already started. This is more than a mere psychological generation of energy. Through the psychological preparation divine grace is working. Grace is at work in and through the natural means a man uses to prepare himself for work. Thus when we pray for peace we are asking God to enable us to be effective peacemakers; when we pray for health we ask that we may make serious and sensible use of the medical means available to us to cure our disease. Our prayer is above all the recognition that there are other influences at work in the matter besides our own. These influences are outside our control but are, like our own, under God's sovereignty. And so we pray that God may work through them as well as through us for the desired effect. Intercessory prayer is the acknowledgment that all depends on God, whether he chooses to work through us, through others, or not at all. The point we are making here, however, is that implicit in our prayer is the recognition that we must work as far as we can for the results we pray for. The important thing is not to use prayer as a quietistic abandonment to Fate or a license to be lazy and leave the work to others. The christian God of both Old and New Testaments is not a deity who works through Fate and acts without the cooperation of his creatures. The God of Creation and Incarnation is a God of partnership and coresponsibility. He helps men by enabling them to help themselves. The success of his creative energy lies in making men succeed in what they pray to do. His answer to our prayers is to make us succeed — not always, of course, in the way we expect.[1]

[1] We are not here considering the problem of our prayers for the success of the efforts of other people in work in which we play no part. That is part of the wider problem of intercessory prayer among the

THE CHRISTIAN AFFIRMATION

In order to understand the place of prayer in christian living it is necessary to call to mind the theological relationship between grace and nature. Grace and nature are not rivals acting on the same level, but partners which come together, each autonomous in its own dimension, to produce a composite result which is at the same time completely natural and completely supernatural. At the practical level this has been well summed by the advice, attributed to St. Ignatius, to pray as if everything depended on God and act as if everything depended on oneself. There is a profound truth enshrined in this aphorism, which when understood goes some way towards clearing the doubts in men's minds caused by the advance of secularization and the apparent demise of prayer. What is dying is not true prayer but a corrupt use of it. True prayer is on the threshold of a new purified existence, as we begin to grasp that

communion of saints, which do do not go into here, except to say, in accordance with the argument of this chapter, that when we pray for other people's work, we do not only ask God to grant success to their efforts (if it be his will) but also we show our willingness to help them if we are called upon to do so. Once again prayer has to be a sign of personal action, not a substitute for it.

it is not an attempt to get results by shortcut methods, but is an existential recognition, *alongside work*, that there is a deeper dimension to this world. This is the dimension of the undergirding all-powerful Creator who is a Mystery to man. Both petition and adoration are means of acknowledging that Mystery as a living fact. By them we deepen our lives because we acknowledge that behind that creation is this Absolute God upon whom everything depends, not least our most active energies and works. Without this deepening we would be living a one-dimensional existence which might well be successful at the superficial level of its own choice, but which could never fulfil man, precisely because there was no acknowledgment of the mastery of God. This deeper fulfilment is only achieved by prayer and adoration.

CHAPTER SIX

Beginnings in Prayer

In this book we have coined the phrase *generative sign for prayer*. It will not have escaped the reader that generative sign has the same meaning as the traditional theological term sacrament. Catholics have always understood by sacrament a sign which not only symbolizes a divine effect but also produces the effect which it is symbolizing. A sacrament in Catholic theology is an *efficacious* symbol, like the pouring of water in baptism which cleanses the soul or the exchange of promises at marriage which effects the union of the two spouses. Efficacious symbol and generative sign are the same thing. Analogously therefore, though in a broader sense than the technical sense used of the sacraments of the Church, prayer can be called a sacrament of the christian life. It shows forth and effects the christian affirmation of living in Christ towards the Father.

THE CHRISTIAN AFFIRMATION

As we saw, prayer is the explicit yes of our christian living which is already an implicit yes to the Father. Prayer is not an escape from living but a symbolic commitment, as it was for Jesus in Gethsemane or Paul in the Arabian desert. It is our "word" given to the Father in Christ. After we have given our word in prayer we live it out in our christian life, and vice versa.

This is a book about personal prayer so we will not dwell on liturgical prayer. Nevertheless this is the place to notice the central importance of the liturgy in christian living. Liturgical prayer, the official prayer of the christian community, is central in christianity because salvation is communal, not individual, since "it has not been God's resolve to sanctify and save men individually, with no regard for their mutual connection, but to establish them as a people, who would give him recognition in truth and service in holiness" (*Lumen Gentium*, Para 9). The most important act of prayer we perform, then, is our joining in the public liturgy of the Church. This is our prime response to God's call. This is the foremost christian response, our first word back to God in reply to his Word to us which saved us and called us. We take our place in the christian assembly and there make our eucharistic prayers of adoration and petition by which we recognize God's sovereignty and fulfil ourselves as baptized christians. We should not think of the liturgy as the prayer we go to after having made our own private personal approaches to God. Rather, we make our first approach in the liturgy as members of the assembly of the baptized and after that, according as the Spirit moves us, we prolong our personal contribution to the communal christian response in our own private prayers. It is not, of course, a question of first in time but of first in importance. Whichever comes first chronologically, the important thing to see is that our private prayer stems from our participation in the public prayer of the Church. The Church mediates grace to us originally in baptism and after that through the Mass and other sacraments. Our private approaches to God are not apart from that mediation but are made from the center of the Church of which we are indebted members before we are active members. This sense that personal prayer is a prolonging of one's public contribution to the liturgy is found in St. Benedict's *Rule*. The communal prayer of the monastery is legislated for in detail and private prayer is regarded as outside legislation. Nevertheless private prayer is spoken of as following on from the communal office, those monks who wish to stay behind after the office for private prayer being encouraged to do so (Ch. 52). In the liturgy are to be found all varieties of approaches the christian assembly makes to God, thanksgiving for our redemption, longing for the coming of Christ, sorrow for our sins, petition for our intentions and adoration. The individual uses this same variety of approaches to God by himself and should see his individual prayer as his personal prolonging of the respective moments in the liturgy when the full assembly made those prayers. Thus, my private prayers of sorrow stem from my participation in the opening liturgy of penance at the beginning of Mass; my thanksgiving prayers are prolongations of the canon; all my worship is a "holding" of that supreme moment of worship at the end of the canon of the Mass, the great doxology, when the full assembly with its priest, gathered together by the Holy Spirit, gives the Father all honor and glory through, with and in Christ. Any personal acts of adoration I make are individual prolongations of that moment in the life of the Church. There is not only a psychological connection between the prayer in private and the liturgy in public, but a theological connection, because of the communal nature of our redemption in Christ.

Since the liturgy of the Church is trinitarian in character, it follows that all personal christian prayer is trinitarian too. This has not always been recognized in the past, but is being so today. The biblical and liturgical movements of this century have awakened christians from a unitarian emphasis on the oneness of the deity in their devotional life. We are seeing more clearly what is implied by the constantly reiterated but not always understood trinitarian phrases with which we always open and close our prayers. Traditionally we have begun praying in the name of the three Persons of the Blessed Trinity but we have tended to go on from there conscious only of a One God listening to our prayers. We have also traditionally ended our prayers through Jesus Christ, in the Spirit, to the Father, but again the full realization of the three Persons of the Trinity and their proper roles in christian worship has been lost. This is not so today. Study of the New Testament shows us that the original followers of Jesus began to pray to the Father in the Spirit through the Son, still alive and reigning beside the Father. The liturgy has preserved these formulas and so has acted as carrier of the original tradition in christian worship down to our own day. It is for us to ponder upon the richness of these formulas and so discover that our prayer is not only our own, but is performed in the power and the name of the Risen Christ. Our poor prayers do not stand on their own but are taken up into the prayer that Christ makes perpetually now at the throne of the Father. He is a human being like ourselves as well as being God, so it is entirely appropriate that our human prayers should be presented to the Father by him. Another way of saying the same thing is to say that Christ within us (subjective christocentricism) prays our prayers, the sap of the Vine rising through them enables the branches to pray with effect. Or again, the work of enabling us to pray can be seen to be the work of the Spirit within us who initiates the whole process and enables us to pray through Christ. "The Spirit too comes to help us in our weakness. For when we cannot choose words in order to pray properly, the Spirit himself expresses our plea in a way that could never be put into words, and God who knows everything in our hearts knows perfectly well what he means, and that the pleas of the saints expressed by the Spirit are according to the mind of God" (Romans 8: 26-7). The "word" of our christian life is best summed up in the one word "Abba" which expresses so intimately our adoption as sons of the Father and brothers and co-heirs of Christ, and it is precisely the work of the Holy Spirit within us to express that word (Gal 4:6-7; Romans 8:14-17). Whether the christian is aware of it or not, he is thoroughly caught up into the Blessed Trinity and cannot in fact make any move as a christian which does not involve the entire Godhead, the Spirit inspiring him to act and pray in the name of Christ to the Father. It is not going too far to suggest that the inner self of the christian is an arena for the Holy Trinity to play out their eternal dialogues of love. The journey inward terminates at the discovery in wonder of the Blessed Trinity dwelling in our hearts. "If anyone loves me he will keep my word, and my Father will love him, and we shall come to him and make our home with him" (John 14:23). We christians, as we go about our daily work, have done more than entertain angels unawares; we are entertaining the Godhead itself.

There are as many ways of praying as

there are people who pray so we will not spend much time considering methods of prayer. Moreover the characteristic of our age among christians is a certain shyness towards method-making in the way we follow Christ and encourage others to follow him. After the post-reformation centuries of keeping to the traditions of the past in an exaggerated way we now react in favor of spontaneity in every christian project we undertake and are suspicious of all blue-prints drawn up prior to action, however experienced the teacher may be. It is an age of authentic commitment, and nowhere more than in prayer is this looked for. It is, however, legitimate to notice that there are two basic approaches to prayer, depending upon whether we start with Life and progress from there to Christ, or whether we start with the Bible and find Christ there. Another way of putting this is to say that since prayer is the christian response to God's word, there are two basic ways of replying corresponding to the two basic ways God speaks to his servants. Firstly God speaks to them in every situation of their daily lives; he is never far from them, constantly calling them to accept his challenge in the various guises it comes to them — this visitor who asks for help, that

telephone which rings, a headache or a be-
reavement. We reply back to God through
this human situation by taking it and offering
it to the Father. It forms the "meat" of our
prayer. We "pray the situation." The eyes of
faith have shown us that this ordinary event
of the day-to-day living contains God, and
we answer back by reaching out with faith
to contact him in it. God's natural word now
in our lives has called forth the reply from
the center of our lives which is our word
back to God. This sort of prayer is a "prayer
of life." But God also speaks to men in the
privileged place which is the Revealed Word
of God, the Bible. Hence a second approach
to praying is to start with a meditative reading of the Word of God in the Bible and
answer back by praying whatever words
come into our minds as a result of reading
the passage from the Bible. Both these ways
of beginning to pray are to be found in
christian tradition. Suffice it to say that they
are clearly complementary, a both-and not
an either-or, because we cannot do without
adverting to either the revealed or the "natural" word of God, and anyway the prayer
that begins at one end will flow towards the
other, and vice versa. We start at the gospel
but our prayer consists in applying what we

read to our lives, so before we finish we have mentally flowed into the realm of daily life. In the same way we start at an event in life which needs to be prayed over, and we discover Christ there, and with him his example and teaching in the New Testament, so we end up at the Bible having begun with life. These two approaches to prayer correspond to the social and gospel inquiry methods of the Young Christian Workers. There the technique of see-judge-act is brought to bear on a situation in the lives of the group and on a passage from the gospel, and it has proved a valuable way of penetrating through an event or gospel passage to Christ. The important thing is not to be rigid in either one or the other approach but to adapt freely according as the mind desires. "Pray the way you can and not the way you can't" (Abbot Chapman).

Everyone who prays begins by using words. It is the way human beings express themselves. If we are faithful about our prayer and are trying to put our whole selves into what we say, the time will come when we feel the need to advance in this journey inward. How is this done? The best way is to begin to lengthen the pauses between the words we say. We keep the same words but space them out with silent pauses which "say it with silence." A pause, for instance, between two phrases of the Lord's Prayer allows the sentiment expressed in the first phrase to sink in and become genuinely part of us before we move on to the next idea and phrase. Said in this way the Lord's Prayer (or any utterance to God) can be made to mean far more than when it is said at speaking pace. There is time to dwell on its sentiments and let them become part of oneself. Taking fifteen minutes to say the Lord's Prayer is more fruitful than taking fifteen seconds. This practice is not for "holy people" but for anyone prepared to try it. We are all children of God and we may be sure that he likes his children to take time and care over their praying to him.

The stage is then set for a further advance in prayer, and again it is not an advance which needs complicated words or very intelligent ideas. It consists simply in the dawning realization that the best prayer of all is the prayer which uses *no words,* because no words are adequate to express all we want to say or can say to God. This kind of praying is when the silent pauses between the words have taken over from the words themselves and mean more, express more, satisfy the pray-er more than any words can. The pause in prayer has now become the prayer, and the words are little more than "coat-hangers" to hang the now-silent prayer on. Praying has become a silent communion, as between two people who know and understand each other well and do not need words to bridge the gap between them. It is the most satisfying and most fulfilling way of praying. It is for all christians. They are all called to enter into close companionship with Jesus. He did not undertake the Incarnation, Death and Resurrection so that his followers should have an uneasy distant sort of relationship with him. He came to enable men to treat him and his Father as close and deep friends. Baptism gives christians the grace to do this. If that is so, it is normal that the prayer of the baptized christian should grow from using words to just being with God in a silence charged with meaning. "Mummy, can I come and sit beside you as you iron?" asked the little girl. She did not want to do anything or say anything in particular. She just wanted to be there. It is normal that prayer for christians should develop towards this child-likeness as we get nearer the Father whose children we all are. The journey inwards is a journey among other things towards simplicity.

In our own day the journey towards simplicity in prayer has a special appeal. In marked contrast to earlier ages people of today prefer simple clean outlines in the things that surround them; the apparatus of living has to be simple. The ages of the baroque and the gothic revivals delighted in complexity and intricate detail. The average victorian house interior, of the sort of architecture which produced St. Pancras Station, shows how highly our fathers rated multiplicity and and variety. A plain thing for them was dull and insufficient; they had to have complexity to express their romantic selves. Perhaps this was because they were basically simple people who believed in themselves and their destiny in a way that the twentieth century cannot. We are more complicated internally than pre-scientific and pre-freudian man, so paradoxically we prefer to be surrounded by simple, unfussy things and have an aversion from clutter in all its manifestations. The contrast between the two ages is mirrored in the field of devotions and prayer. The Romantic Age in the Catholic Church produced a devotional life of variety and complexity. Prayers like the Thirty Days' Prayer or the

Novena to Our Lady of Perpetual Succor, devotions like that to the Nine First Fridays, a multiple appeal to the saints, prayer books which piled on the words and the different ways of approaching God, all manifested this love of the complex and various. Without this multiplicity of ascetical practices those Catholics would not have been helped to love God and serve their neighbor. Not surprisingly it was an age when mysticism was not attractive and was considered rather suspect. That is changed now, and today's Catholics cannot settle down to the prayers or devotions of their fathers which seem to them to say too much and to be spiritually indecent. What was a help in the past is no longer a help but a hindrance. Nowadays we prefer a simple approach. It is a common experience to find that people pass quickly to praying in the silent, simple fashion described above. Rather than say prayers and have devotions, they prefer to pray and be devoted. There has been a shift in emphasis from the ornate and complex to the plain and the simple. Other things being equal, this is surely a movement in the direction of the gospel, which was essentially a call to be simple and uncomplicated.

There is another kind of simplicity which

is close to the gospel and which is not a matter of temperament but of intention. This is the simplicity which comes from poverty of spirit. It is the first fruit of a serious approach to prayer. Simply put, poverty of spirit means making no conditions to one's loving surrender to God. So often we say to God that we want to give our whole lives to him, but there are hidden reservations in this self-giving which work in the opposite direction to the direction of the prayer. Our hearts do not completely follow our lips. These reservations are "riches" which hinder us from going straight to God in the journey inward and consequently are the opposite of poverty of spirit. They are unnecessary baggages which weigh us down in the journey and which have to be discarded before we can proceed further. In this journey only if we travel light will we make progress. Sometimes these reservations to our surrender to God are material riches; we find ourselves saying we will love God as long as we have this or that thing or are left in comfort and security till we die. But there are more subtle and hidden reservations to true christian living than those. We can have mental riches in the shape of prejudices which hinder us in our abandonment to God; we cannot give up certain ideas or ways of doing things and cling to these with more tenacity than we cling to Truth. Such obstacles to christian openness are particularly discernible in an age of ecclesial transition like our own. The fresh winds blowing through the Church reveal not a few christians who hold on to contingent positions with more zeal than they cling to the Absolute God. Another such set of reservations to being open to God can be our attitude to people; we can be notably possessive about certain persons and draw them to ourselves in a way that excludes God and eventually destroys the other person. All these attitudes tend against a complete surrender to God and if not checked can turn christian endeavor from service of others into self gratification. They are seldom explicit, of course, and have to be discovered in ourselves as we go along. The adventure of christian living often consists in spotting these unseen obstacles and then rooting them out of our lives. In other words before we can say yes unreservedly to God in Christ we have to have spotted our inclination to say "yes, but . . ." in all its forms, and be ruthless with ourselves about it.

If we are courageous about the ridding ourselves of the internal desire to possess created things for self and turn them to our own advantage the result will be not a diminishment of love for persons and things but an increased, cleansed love of them. Christian detachment does not lead to puritanism — the loss of love for this world — but to a much truer love of the world, the sort of love for all things that St. Francis showed, which was a direct result of his poverty of spirit. St. Francis had no designs for himself on the world. He had achieved the grace of having no "but's" in his surrender to the Father. He was thus liberated from the tyranny of human possessiveness and had reached that condition of complete simplicity which is the goal of living according to the beatitudes. He took life as it came to him as a gift from God and made no demands in return. This was possible for him because his surrender to God was unconditional; it was a total commitment with no taking back with the left hand what he had given with his right hand. Looking at the lives of the saints, we do well to warn ourselves, with the poet, that such a condition of complete simplicity does not come easily but costs "not less than everything." We need the drive and force of the Holy Spirit within us to keep us persevering towards this goal, for without that we would scarcely face in the right direction, let alone travel along the road. It is a road all followers of Christ have to follow, and one that ought to have a particular appeal to modern men in their desire for simple living and internal freedom — if it were not so difficult.

CHAPTER SEVEN

Knowing and Loving Ourselves

There are few greater caricatures of what it means to be a christian than the wide-spread idea that it means having no emotions, being a stoical character ready with a stiff upper lip to cope with the vicissitudes of life. We can plainly see that this is wrong if we stop to think of the kind of person Jesus Christ was. The angry man who picked up a cord to drive the buyers and sellers out of the temple, who wept in sadness over Jerusalem, who was bathed in a sweat of fear before his arrest was not a stoical, emotionless man, and obviously his followers did not think they ought to be emotionless either, since they portrayed him in the gospels with all those feelings. It was only later under non-biblical influence that the idea crept into christianity that christians ought to do away with their emotions and live with-

out them. It is not in the New Testament.
What *is* in the New Testament is the idea
that the emotions are there to be used and
controlled in the service of Christ but not re-
pressed. Poverty of spirit, the spirit of the
beatitudes, is the ideal set before all followers of Christ by St. Paul and the evangelists
but it does not mean having no emotions. It
means being free from their tyranny and
therefore able to use them uninhibitedly and
without fear. Poverty of spirit is freedom in
the use and enjoyment of the emotions and
not their repression. The emotions are in fact
the raw material of all human living. They
form the stuff of our daily lives. From moment to moment we are attracted passion-
ately to people, repelled by others, angry,
bored, bursting with joy, trembling with fear,
filled with a sense of uneasiness, sad, content. Our whole day is filled with these reactions; it is what being a man or woman
means, and to try to do away with these feelings would be to opt out of being a human
being. So vivid are the emotions that it is not
even enough to say that we *have* them; it is
truer to say we *are* them while they last, as
everyone can testify, especially those who
are blessed by being emotional. Emotional
people are more human than those with

weak emotions. The latter lack a strength that the former have. Jesus was intensely emotional.

The emotions of man, however, are not the whole of his life. They are instinctual, pre-voluntary, the stuff out of which men make their decisions. This is where poverty of spirit comes in. It implies a control over the emotions which makes it possible for the follower of Jesus Christ to channel his strong instinctive reactions in the direction of love of God and men because he is able to resist the temptation to sink beneath them and let them lead him anywhere. He controls them, not they him. In other words, the emotions have to be directed by the mind and will of man, which alone are capable of choosing the right goals for those instinctive reactions. Given strong emotions (as in Jesus of Nazareth) it is, then, necessary to exercise an even stronger human direction over these drives, otherwise one who is already an emotional man will become a merely animal man, reacting automatically to every stimulus. The attraction of Jesus was obviously in the fact that both his head and his heart were intensely human, but his power came from the fact that the head controlled the heart. He knew what he was about. His pity, meekness, anger, joy were not only the immediate reactions of a vibrant human being. They were also the consciously directed reactions of a dutiful son about his Father's business. If we try to imitate this we will begin to see how to live with our emotions and avoid the twin dangers of either being a slave to them (and consequently only partly human) or being dry and emotionless (and consequently only partly human). Avoiding both these dangers will mean being glad that we have feelings but even gladder that we control them and direct them to christian goals. In this way we will not feel guilty, either about being emotional or about being being strict with ourselves in the use of those emotions. It need scarcely be said that this is a hard task. Yet the existence of the saints shows that those who buckle down to imitating Christ in their lives achieve this apparently impossible balance. St. Teresa of Avila using all her femininity to promote the reform of the carmelites in 16th century Spain, moving among prelates, princes and nuncios with unashamed charm and guile, or Pastor Bonhoeffer writing those letters so full of feeling and humanity from a nazi prison, show that by aiming at Christ the balance can be achieved. The result is a willed serenity —

not the serenity of a cabbage with no emotions, but the serenity of someone who is fully human and emotional but remains tranquil beneath and through the emotional storms at the surface of his being; someone, in other words, who has a God-given calm at the center of his personality where is to be found the "still point of the turning world." Such a calm comes only from being possessed by a poverty of spirit which does not seek to dominate and grasp good things for self but is serene in the knowledge that God is our Father and holds all things in his hand. It is a realization which is the first fruit of prayer and comes by grace rather than human achievement, a grace, however, which is there for all who really want it.

The second fruit of prayer is self knowledge. Men achieve knowledge of themselves by relating to other people. Shut up in their own rooms, leading lives apart from other people, men do not develop any real knowledge of themselves; they tend to be deceived more and more by their own fancies and self-projections. The dictators of history were surrounded by sycophants who never told them the truth and lived virtually alone because there was no real meeting with another in their lives. As a result they ended up completely duped about themselves, believing any kind of bizarre fiction as long as it redounded to their credit. This is a parable of what can happen to any of us if we stay apart from our fellow men and refuse a genuine meeting with others. For it is in meeting and working with others that we come to know ourselves. This happens often because our colleagues tell us quite bluntly what is wrong with us. However, quite apart from whether our friends are candid ones who tell us what they think of us, we reach an understanding of ourselves by reflecting on our reactions to communal life — to new ideas which threaten our comfort, for instance, or to the way in which we react to the success of a rival or to the growth of independence in a child. In all the hundred and one ways in which we bump up against others we grow in knowledge not only of these others whom we are meeting but also of ourselves who are doing the meeting. Self knowledge comes from the encounter with others.[1]

It is, however, the encounter with the

---

[1] Those who have taken part in "sensitivity groups" will bear this out. Out of the intense awareness of the feelings of other people comes a parallel awareness of one's own feelings, hitherto only partially known.

Other who is God, in prayer, which provides the fullest and most formidable kind of self knowledge. If our prayer is genuinely a meeting with the Reality of the Father and not just a form of preoccupation with self, then we should not be surprised to find that it brings with it a rather frightening disclosure of ourselves to ourselves. As we grow nearer to God in prayer we begin to see ourselves as God sees us. Of course the full sight of ourselves through the eyes of God is not possible for men, but as prayer brings us nearer to God we begin to be illumined by his divine light and come to see our lives in the perspective of God, not self. This is not a "holy" happening with shafts of light or divine illuminations, still less is it a matter of visions and revelations; it is, on the contrary, a dull humdrum affair as our daily lives are progressively revealed to us as mean and mediocre. The insufficiency of our motives, our mixed intentions, our basic self-centeredness show up with uncomfortable clarity and we are faced with the discovery of ourselves as corrupt and sinful. Sometimes this realization comes to us in prayer, sometimes outside prayer in a remark from another or in the privacy of our family lives. In whatever way it comes to us, the connection is clear. We see ourselves more clearly, *because* we are pursuing a life of prayer which opens out to us the perspective of God and saintliness. In that light we are shown up for what we really are.

The paradoxical fact about this self discovery is that just because we have prayed, and so come closer to God, we begin to see ourselves as "further away than ever from God." This is not, of course, the case, but it seems like that. What has happened is that we have begun to see faults in ourselves which were there all along but which we lacked the insight into self to see before. If you bring the sleeve of your coat up to a light the spots of dust and dirt which are on it will be seen for the first time. Bringing your sleeve to the light has not caused the dirt to be there, only caused it to be seen. So it is with the faults of the man who prays. This provides one of the tests for beginners in the life of prayer: to get through the trial of discovering themselves to be apparently worse just when they hoped they would be finding themselves better. It has to be pointed out to them that this revelation of their faults is a step forwards not backwards, and if handled humbly will be therapeutic to their christian endeavor, not destructive of it.

118

KNOWING AND LOVING OURSELVES

To be therapeutic, this experience has to be received with humility. The proud man will react against the discovery of his faults and try to pretend they are not there in one way or another — often by blaming other people for them ("I failed my exams because of the educational system"). The humble man will be realistic and simply accept what he sees, neither indulging in exaggerated self hate nor in an operation to sweep his faults under the carpet. He will calmly accept the discovery of his hitherto hidden faults — pride, duplicity, basic laziness, lurking impurity and so on — and see that without grace he cannot hope to improve but that with grace he can. There will be no indignation with himself, but the undergirding, inspiring Force, God, will enable him to improve. The experience of the sight of self as rotten is not meant to make us have recourse to the Deus ex machina who will heal us without our efforts, but to lead us to the christian reaction to correct our faults "as if everything depended on ourselves" and to pray about that operation "as if everything depended on God."

Perhaps the most important lesson that is learned in this experience is a lesson in honesty. We discover ourselves in the light of truth and do not flinch from the sight; instead, we accept it in humility and tranquillity. The scales fall from our eyes, scales which have accumulated from birth because of the atmosphere of falsehood and dishonesty prevalent in our industrial, commercial society. We are all, in a sense, educated by society to be salesmen of ourselves (President Kennedy wore spectacles in private but never in public; Hitler had a special typewriter constructed with big letters so that he could read all documents before him without outsiders knowing that he was nearsighted) so this uncomfortable experience of the death of the salesman within ourselves has to happen if we are to grow in truth. The experience is a liberating one if we have the courage to go through with it. Instead of being disillusioned and giving up in pride (all discouragement stems from pride) we quietly carry on, knowing now experientially that "without God we can do nothing." We find ourselves using formulas of humility and contrition and *meaning* them almost for the first time. It becomes actually true that we are sinners! Or that we need grace! There is now no make-believe in our prayers. This is a liberation and brings with it a sense of expansion, because we see now that we are living and praying in the light of reality. We look back to earlier days before we realized our sinfulness with relief that they are past and that the falsity of our former self-knowledge has been enlightened. In Jesus' parable of the pharisee and publican at prayer, the pharisee came away from the temple more constricted than ever in his inner life. He was one of the Just, so he had to defend even to himself an image of perfection which was bound to lead to further insecurity and fear — the life of a salesman is increasingly anxious. But the publican went home free and happy in the knowledge that he had no false image to defend or any part to play before the world except the part of being simply himself. This is an expanding experience. In jungian terms it is the experience of accepting the Shadow and withdrawing the Persona. It is the first step towards individuation. It is possible for all christians who begin to pray and are led in the light of God to see themselves as they really are and to accept that sight. It is the fruit of prayer taken seriously. In prayer we place ourselves face to face with Reality and Truth in the person of God. Little wonder, then, that the result is the painful experience of discovering ourselves as we really are. It is true that all encounters bring self knowledge, but the encounter in prayer with God who is Truth itself is clearly the most effective. That is why the act of prayer is so necessary for the christian. Without it he will not grow in self knowledge and will end up falling into the temptation of all sincerely religious people, which is to pursue self perfection at the expense of others and in the name of religion. This is pharisaism. The appalling sight of self as imperfect, which is the fruit of prayer, is the remedy for this, for it makes us relinquish the pursuit of self perfection and simply cling to the person of God the Father.

From what has been said above it will be obvious that the way the christian reacts to the sight of himself as sinful is even more important than the sight itself. If the man is a proud man, he will not accept what he sees but simply reject the whole experience in any number of ways from being "too busy to stop and think" to projecting it on to others like "It's the fault of the system." All these ways of rejecting truth are cowardly and dishonest. They are automatic reactions of fear, and stem from the lack of emotional control discussed at the beginning of this chapter. On the other hand the man who has the grace of poverty of spirit will be able to accept the sight of himself as a sinner because he does not conduct his life on the lines of defending a public image of perfection or any other such "richness," but is happy to be brought low by God and made poor. Another way of putting this is to say that it is important to replace the wrong sort of self-love with the right sort of self-love in the pursuit of Christ. The sight of self as sinful takes the form of seeing oneself as self-centered, selfish, ego-inflated, proud. This way of loving self is wrong because untrue — we are not the center of the universe; God is. The temptation, however, on receipt of this illumination, is to react towards self-hate. This is, in fact, only another form of pride. What Christ desires is for us to accept ourselves as valuable in ourselves, and be sorry not for what we basically are but for the mess we have made of what we are. What we basically are, are valuable persons, created in God's image and redeemed by Christ's love. We are immensely valuable and important persons in God's eyes. He loves us! Our sorrow for sin therefore should take the form of sorrow for what we have done, never of sorrow for what we are. This is not easy, for it means facing up to our future possibilities in the midst of the shame of knowing that we have misused past ones. It requires humility to go on believing that we can improve, to face God as sinners and ask to start again. It is easier to run away in despair and say that we are too bad to improve. This gives us a crumb of comfort in subtle pride. Judas did this when he realized what his betrayal of Jesus implied. He went and hanged himself in lonely despair. Peter, on the same night realized that he had betrayed his Master, but did not give way to despair, though surely he was tempted to after all his boasting. He had the courage to go back and say he was sorry, face to face with Jesus. In doing so, he learned to love himself.

The man who loves himself can love other people because he has a firm base from which to do so. The man who is not sure of his own worth will be constantly seeking to establish it in his own eyes. He will try to do this in his relations with other people, either by trying to ingratiate himself with them (to show himself that he is loved) or by retiring into splendid isolation (to show himself he does not need other people). All these common reactions in society stem from an inability to love self; they are people's ways of trying to cope with a feeling of inadequacy. Some people cannot agree with anyone but have to quarrel in a spirit of contradiction; this is because they feel inadequate if they are not winning an argument or if they are falling in with someone else's views; they do not love themselves enough to feel easy in agreement. Others cannot disagree with anyone; this is usually because they feel threatened by disagreement — it means to them that people do not love them. The third kind of self-hate is the cultivation of impassivity in isolation from communication with others; this too can be caused by lack of self love and the need to prove one's worth to oneself by doing without human company. The result of all these inadequacies is the sad one that a real relationship with the other person is impossible since the relationship with others is being used for establishing the value of self instead of for loving the other person. Only when the value of self has been taken for granted can a real relationship with the other be possible. Jesus Christ knew that we have to love self before we can begin to love others; he said we ought to love our neighbors "as ourselves." It was an important insight, and one which has to be remembered by the maturing christian when he comes to the stage of seeing himself as rotten and sinful. This is the moment for him to be ruthless in rooting out selfishness but to be careful to replace this wrong sort of love of self with the right sort, not with self hate, which is psychologically so harmful. "Love thyself" is good christian advice, not a dangerous call to hedonism. It means accepting oneself for what one is, physique, talents, possibilities and all, and from that firm base going out to love all other people, whether their reaction to this is love, hate, indifference or enthusiasm. Christian love begins at home and extends from there to the ends of the world.

The sacrament of self awareness and self love is confession. In this sacrament the christian endeavor is to know oneself as one really is and to love oneself for Christ's sake is taken up and sanctified. More is involved in the sacrament of penance than the forgiving of sins, because when we meet Jesus Christ in judgment he is concerned with more than merely forgiving us. He is the shepherd of our souls and so desires to heal us and care for us in the future. As we have seen, this healing and care of our innermost selves means a growth in knowledge of ourselves and an increase in proper self love. The sacrament of confession should therefore be an experience of self awareness and self love as well as being an experience of forgiveness. This medicinal aspect of confession has always been recognized in theory, but nullified in practice by the concrete shape of the sacrament, the dark, narrow box, the grill of anonymity, the disembodied voice of the priest. Without wishing to do away with the quick confession of absolution in the box, we ought to seek to develop this sacrament on parallel lines so that for those who wish it can become a genuine experience of understanding and growth in love. This sacrament will surely develop in the future into something more personal where the priest and penitent know each other and have a relationship over the months which is genuinely pastoral at the same time as being sacramental. In other words we ought to develop our use of this sacrament into an event of spiritual counselling, the penitent teling his sins against the whole background of his life of christian commitment, and the priest helping out with sympathetic listening and questioning and mutually agreed advice, where necessary, at the end, which then leads on to absolution. In this way all that we have said in this chapter about knowing oneself as one is in the eyes of God is taken into account and used in a perfectly natural way between penitent and priest who trust each other, and is then made supernatural by the sacramental word; it means that the spiritual experience of growing in self knowledge is situated in the middle of the sacrament instead of being permitted for an eccentric few outside the sacrament, linked intentionally and no more. Our growth in christian self awareness like all spiritual increase does in fact spring from the sacraments; it is therefore proper to make this be seen and enacted in the sacrament of confession. In recent years the frequency of going to confession has decreased among catholics. This is not good if it means that we are thinking less about sins and are less concerned to do anything about them. But the decrease in quantitative use of the sacrament might be a good thing if it were accompanied by using it as we have outlined above. Many christians would say that this is precisely what is happening; there is a widespread desire to make the sacrament more personal and pastorally helpful, which is initially taking the form all over the Church of going less to confession in the old anonymous way. But in places where priests are providing really helpful "pastoral" confessions, armchair to armchair in dialogue rather than through the grill in monologue, there is a notable expansion of the use of this sacrament. It looks like a movement of the Holy Spirit in the Church today.

CHAPTER EIGHT

The Transformation
of Prayer

The trouble with books about spiritual life is that they tend to give the impression that spiritual growth depends only on the efforts of man so that by the time the reader arrives at the end of the book, the movement of God whereby he sweeps men off their feet — the phenomenon which appears in the Bible as so many violent happenings, Jacob wrestling, David dancing, Paul being flung off his horse, the mighty wind of the Holy Spirit in the Acts of the Apostles — is submerged under a careful construction of human advice. When this happens you have a prime example of Hamlet without the prince: a book about the work of God in the soul of the christian which ignores the work of God in

131

favor of the works of man. It is understandable how this happens. It is, surely, a safety precaution to prevent the followers of Christ from "leaving it all to grace" and ending up with a quietistic version of christian living which portrays God as working without the cooperation of man. As we saw in Chapter 5 this is to promote grace at the expense of nature, an error which the advance of secularization has exposed for what it is, namely a misunderstanding of what the Bible means by creation and redemption. Nevertheless once it has been said that man must work with God in the work of christian growth and therefore spiritual books ought to contain plenty of human advice, it is still necessary to point out that God himself does not always observe human laws of growth and is liable to advance upon anyone as a mighty wind and sweep him off his feet, leaving his careful spiritual construction in ruins. When this happens conversion takes place. There is enough evidence in the history of christian spirituality from biblical times to remind us never to forget that it does happen. At all times and in all versions of christianity there has been this phenomenon of conversion. Rosemary Haughton has made a study of this for modern christians in three books[1] using both literary and biblical evidence and correlating these with modern experience. She points out that even though for many christians conversion is slow and gradual and not a spectacular Road to Damascus experience, there is an element of jerk and jolt in every christian conversion, an element of surprise, as the process of steady formation gives way to the unpredictable grace of transformation. She sees the human preparation for the Spirit as a process of formation in which all the laws of christian education ought to be followed; but the important moment is the moment of transformation when human prudence is no longer adequate and when what is required of the christian is simply a courageous surrender to the Holy Spirit. When this happens, the christian discovers that he is being asked to do things he never dreamed of doing and think thoughts he never thought before, in obedience to Christ. It is a moment of real growth, which combines both an element of continuity with the process of formation which led up to it, and an element of complete discontinuity due to the overmastering grace of God.

[1] On Trying To Be Human (1966), The Transformation Of Man (1967), Act of Love (1968).

One of the features of christian conversion is the coming together of those two aspects of christian life which ought always to be one but which at the beginning of the christian commitment are separated in the mind of most people: prayer and life. We have said (in Chapter 4) that the relation between them is that prayer is the generative sign of life. At the beginning, this connection is a theoretical one; we have to make it in our minds before it is obvious to us. At the point of christian growth we are now considering, this connection between prayer and living becomes plain; there is a coalescing of the two, so that living is seen to be praying and prayer is seen to be living. There is no need to make the connection. It makes itself. We clearly see that when we go about our daily duties we are relating to the Father (that is, praying) and that when we stand before the Father in prayer we are indubitably performing a christian duty (that is, working). Those feelings of guilt and insecurity which often attack christians and make them feel when they are doing something that they ought to be doing something else, and especially when they are praying they ought to be performing something "useful," now drop away and are experienced as a threat no more. The christian is now aware that praying is a supremely authentic part of his relationship to the Father and he no longer feels apologetic about it, but just *prays*. Love has made him forget to theorize and he happily spends hours in prayer for no other reason than that God is to be loved. A notable feature of conversion is the felt need to pray at length before the Father; it is an experience of complete fulfilment which the christian undergoes when he finds time in the center of his life to pray for an hour or two at a stretch. The old pseudo arguments that this is a waste of time or that life itself is all the prayer we need or that only monks should indulge in long praying reappear as surface bothers from time to time but they no longer have much force, since love has now taken over. Love, after all, does not speak the language of minimum necessity but of maximum possibility. God is supremely adorable, supremely *matters,* and therefore to spend time in pure prayer needs no defense. The least effective argument against praying is, therefore, the argument that it is a waste of time, because this is precisely what people in love want to do: to waste time in each other's company! The most effective expression of love is in fact the squandering of time between lover and beloved, and it is a matter for considerable suspicion to find a lover who looks at the clock and resents time spent in his beloved's company. It is the same with the man of prayer. A call to prodigality in the giving of time to prayer comes over him. To be generous in time spent in prayer appears as the most meaningful way of being generous to God. He gladly gives up sleep or recreation in order to find time to pray. If he did not, or argued against it on the grounds of its being an escape, he would begin to suspect his sincerity. Praying is the direct and obvious way of expressing the love which is possessing him at the center of his being and which must overflow somehow. And because prayer is a sign of life and not an escape from it, he sees his prayer as the force which urges him to christianize every moment of his life and go out with equal generosity to his neighbor in love. A modern figure who symbolizes this urge to pray and whose prayer made him available to all comers is Charles de Foucauld. In his little hermitage at Tamanrasset in the heart of the Sahara he had at one end his altar where he prayed four or five hours a day. But in the middle of the baked clay house, beside the door, he had his chair where he sat and received all those who came to see him. Here he was available to everyone whenever they called, and so open was he to the needs of his callers, whether they were poor Tuaregs or important French officials, that he became known as the Universal Brother. His being available to the Father for hours at a stretch in prayer made him available to the Son in his brothers who interrupted him when they called. This double availability which at heart is a single availability is the symbol of the place of prayer in the life of a committed christian.

Transformed prayer is simple prayer. It prefers silence to words. It does not need methods or any complicated "apparatus." It is an expression of faith rather than religion, that is, it contacts God directly in love and trust and is unconcerned about methodic inmediaries. People who see a marvellous view through a window have got beyond busying themselves with the glass in the window. They look out in wonder. That is how we pray. It is notoriously difficult to describe a simple thing like personal prayer because it *is* so simple, and also so personal to each one who prays. However, at the risk of being flat-footed and once-removed from experience, we could say that the prayer of one who has been transformed by the grace of conversion is deeper, simpler, more passive and God-centered than the prayer of those who are beginning to form themselves. The moment of grace makes our yes to God come alive in a wonderful way which is ineffable at the time but which later analysis can show to have those four qualities.

Transformed prayer is deep. It takes place at a level of our being which is clearly not the surface one of feelings and distractions. Attempts have been made to describe this area of our personality where contemplative prayer takes place. Earlier generations preferred to call it a higher area than the ordinary one of everyday decisions, for instance the "fin point de l'âme" of the seventeenth century french writers. But (all this is frankly metaphor) moderns prefer the image of depth to that of height. Spiritual progress is a journey inward; we go deeper as we advance towards God, penetrating to areas where unconscious as well as conscious forces are at work. Thus prayer is now an operation conducted below the imagination and feeling level. It goes on beneath and through all surface activity. Prayer which uses pictures and appeals to the senses is found no longer possible; there has been a drying up of the sources at that level. Prayer is now a matter of what the mind and heart can do, a deep giving at the center of our being, which is simultaneously part of our daily living and in touch with eternity. It is a deep engagement of the ground of our being with God himself which affects our whole active personality at source. What happens to our emotions and feelings during this? The wise man uses sops to keep them "with" rather than "against" what is going on at the deeper center of the self. Such sops as a crucifix, darkness, the sanctuary lamp, a picture, words and phrases have proved useful at times to different people. These sops do not constitute the prayer itself but help to "carry" it. We cannot really do without them because we are men, not angels, and the attempt to be the latter is always disastrous. However, the real activity of prayer is going on at that "level of our being which is deeper than the intellect, more personal than feelings, more human than the subconscious. It is the level on which the unity of the two great aspects of our being, knowledge and love, exists. There man's effort to lay hold of truth is inseparable from his striving after goodness. In this primal unity, knowledge is not a cold light and love is not a blind urge.

139

Knowledge is full of love and love itself has vision" (*Dutch Catechism*, page 125).

The main conscious shift in the transformation of prayer is that it becomes more simple. No longer does the imagination picture and the mind argue and discourse. Mind and will together, the primal unity of man, stand still before the marvellous fulness of God's mystery; they dwell, as one does before a panoramic view, or with a friend. If there is any movement, it is circular, around mystery. It is not a question of making different acts of approach to God, but of pausing and saying "abba" or some short word which acts as the vehicle of all our acts. In other words, prayer becomes an act of intuition. The preliminaries are now presumed; there is no need for meditative considerations of truths already known; we begin to intuit as soon as we start to pray and stay that way. Because God has revealed himself as personal, Father, Son and Spirit, this intuitive prayer can be described as the growth in personal relationship with him from stranger to friend to lover. Silence is now experienced as the best form of communication with God, whereas before silence tended to be a breakdown in communication, as it is between strangers. We pass from knowing about God by studying him in the Bible and Church to knowing him in the personal contact of intuition here and now. It is theology in the older sense of the term, knowing God by personal relationship. Because it is an act of simple apprehension this prayer gets described in metaphors of the senses. These comparisons are helpful as long as it is remembered that they are metaphors and that in prayer, which is an act of faith, we do not really "see" or "hear" God. Thus this prayer is called contemplative, or listening to God, or waiting on God. In fact what these metaphors are trying to say is that prayer is extremely simple, and the simplicity takes the form of *active passivity*; we are wholly active and alert, but apparently doing nothing. It can be very tiring. It is how lovers pass the time.

As we grow deeper and more simple in our prayer we are also more conscious of the passivity in it, that is, of being drawn forward by God, or perhaps even being pushed along from behind! Whether we experience prayer as a drawing or a pushing the fact is that this experience is a growth in understanding of Reality, because that is what christian theology tells us to be true: God draws us; he first loved us, not we him, and all prayer is simply the response of the christian to a prior initiative on God's part, not an approach from man's side. To think it is the latter, is to be wrong, out of touch with Reality. It is helpful sometimes to change our image of God as the God Above to that of the God Ahead, because the biblical idea of God is of One who acts in history and who continues to act through historical events all of which will culminate one day in his final Act of History when he comes again. There is a constant movement forward: we are not only living under the all-seeing providence of God but also travelling towards the final revelation of the mystery of our salvation when Christ comes again. And prayer is especially the act whereby we look forward and *long,* an act of being drawn by God forward, watching and waiting for the God who will soon come, straining with an eager longing in our hearts "more than watchman for daybreak" (Ps 129). This, too, explains the simplicity of prayer, for one does not act busily as one waits for someone to come; one makes all necessary preparations and then simply *waits.* It is, of course, important to remember that the quiet simplicity of prayer is not the end itself of praying but the means by which we pray. If we forget that, we fall into the mistakes of the Quietists who turned Quiet into the aim and object of their praying instead of its being the way in which we contact God. God alone is the adequate aim and object of prayer, and to make the object anything other than him is to be guilty of subtle self cultivation and not to be committed to the service of God. This explains why the true mystics of christianity have often been most active men and women even while their prayer was quiet and tranquil. Because they did not make the quiet and tranquillity the aim of life but only a means towards resting in God's will they were able to be thoroughly active and hectic when they had to, without loss of their deep-down peace. This deep-down peace amidst surface strife is surely the peace that Jesus promised his followers. It was not to be like what the world gives but was the fruit of complete poverty of spirit in the middle of action. It was a positive attitude and not a mere negative cessation of activity.

Lastly, prayer grows in us when the whole of our christian affirmation becomes intensely God-centered. We lose consciousness of ourselves and become conscious only of God. This is an important transition because once again it marks a growth towards reality in our praying. Beginners nearly always center their prayers around themselves or around the means they use to pray (the liturgy, formula of prayer, rosary, etc.) and so in the very act of praying cease to reach out to contact God and only contact the *means*; looking out of the window they concentrate on the glass, not the view, and so they do not use those prayers with complete authenticity. A transition is needed. This is the transition of becoming absorbed in the Reality of God, a transition from "religion" (self-centered) to faith (God-centered). In this kind of prayer the whole apparatus of religion disappears from consciousness and GOD expands to fill everything. Self disappears too, for God is the whole content of reality at this point. At this stage the man who prays comes up against the "felt experience" of the mystics of the infinite gap between what we say about God, and God himself. Human terms are now felt as totally inadequate if applied to God, and yet they are the only terms we have. We have always given a mental assent to the fact that our knowledge of God is at best analogical and not univocal. At this stage of conversion we now feel it in the very depths of our being. We realize with pain, and frustration at times, that the ideas and the words of our God-talk are of "not God" and never can portray God as he really is. So we are left this side of the barrier, baffled and sterile, yet somehow also at peace. We are at peace because our faith tells us, even as it is baffled, that this is the authentic way for men to meet God, and that in the former days when we thought we knew God and understood him we were even more remote from him than now when we experience our conceptual inadequacy. It is good to know that the cloud of unknowing in which we stumble around is nearer to the Reality which is Truth than our earlier clarity which shames us now with its shallow certainties. Prayer has brought us to a state of standstill, but we are surprised to find a deep contentment in the bafflement because somehow we are also conscious that our love can pass through the barrier which our mental powers cannot surmount. It is difficult to put this into words, but there is distinct experience of contacting God by love in the midst of the experience of being unable to contact him with knowledge. We reach out and touch God in loving faith, surrendering to him even though we cannot grasp him in knowledge. "By love may he be gotten and holden but by thought never," was how the medieval writer put it. So the bafflement of prayer is also a kind of loving contact with God. This bewilderment is good for us, since it is a purification of all conceit in our approach to God. Our proud selves find themselves drawn towards the one reality which is worth knowing but they cannot master it. The Creator God is everywhere, but is essentially unknowable by human beings because they are too small for him. God masters men, not they him. Recognizing that fact existentially is prayer.

Christians should never forget the wide gap that exists between the language they use to describe God and the reality of God himself. It is in fact an infinite gap. Good theologians (as opposed to mere controversialists) are conscious of it all the time. They have to use human language about God and his purposes but their use of those terms taken from human experience points beyond the terms to mystery. Karl Rahner testifies: "It is not only the right but the duty of theology to allow this gulf to be sensed ever more keenly, to refer men from the apparent clarity of its conceptions to the blinding brilliance of mystery which seems to us to be darkness." If we understand this we will understand why so much theologizing takes the form of iconoclasm. Our human ideas and conceptions about the way God works have to be constantly renewed through history as man's way of understanding himself and his world develops. This means breaking old conceptions and forming new ones. Thus ideas like redemption, atonement, transmitted original sin — even, for some, the word God — are no longer helpful for many moderns, so they have to be thrown out ruthlessly and new ideas forged. In this way a new theology, true to tradition but relevant to the new insights into man and the world which have been gained, will slowly emerge. It will not be a quick or easy task, and when it is completed christians will have to resist the temptation to think the new concepts are any more permanent or less contingent than the old concepts. The process is not one of producing a new set of absolutes to replace an old set, but of producing a new set of infinitely inadequate models of the inconceivable God which happen to be more useful for our age than the old ones.

Faced, therefore, with the apparently wild talk of theologians the non-theologian has to keep calm in his bewilderment and ask himself whether that which is going on is the rejection of God and the Bible or merely the rejection of former ways of talking about God. This is the important difference. If it is indeed the former that is happening, then we are faced with atheism plain and simple, which is scarcely a valid course for the follower of Christ. If, however, all that is being rejected are older ways of talking about God together with the whole ethos surrounding them, then it is a question of an agnosticism which may well be deeply christian and biblical. For most modern christians it is surely the latter that is the case. Not God but the traditional approach to God is dead for them. This radical agnosticism (which must be followed by creative thinking) is not only necessary in the field of catechetics — the communication of christianity in a form which is relevant to the world today — but, more important, it is deeply necessary in itself for the understanding of God. It is an inevitable fruit of the contemplative approach to God, being a deepening of our relationship to God in Christ; a movement forward, not backward. To pull back, therefore, from the painful process of having our former images shattered is to pull back from God himself. None have been more agnostic about God than the great theologians and saints; they had the courage to let their childhood images be broken and with them a whole way of following Christ; it was that which made them saints. The man who is drawn into prayer by God will be asked to face this experience too. Sooner or later he must let his ideas about God, precious and helpful at one time in his formation, be broken in order to allow the transformation of grace to take place in him. No one can chart or plan when this ought to happen, though the evidence is that it happens early to contemporary man in his search for God. All that can be done is to be ready for it when it happens and then allow God room to move amidst the ruins. If, with God's grace, we do that, then we may be sure that our agnosticism is a creative, not sterile, one. In the mysterious workings of God's love in this world the best contribution man can make to the creative work of the Father is to be radically agnostic and completely poor in spirit. This prevents his obscuring the simplicity of the gospel by absolutizing the transitory structures of christian theology and churchmanship. The most effective way to do this is by prayer, for prayer better than anything else exposes us to the purifying fire of God's creative love. It opens us to God, the Absolute, and in his light we are emptied of merely human notions about this world and God. There is no better program for a radical christian, and there is no other way to God.

CHAPTER NINE

The Relevance of Mystery

There are two kinds of questions that can be asked of life: "how" questions and "whether" questions. The first kind of question is asked by people who accept the system they are working within and are only concerned to make it work well, so they ask how this is to be done and what kinds of improvement can be made to it; they are also concerned about how they can personally adjust to it. The second kind of questioners are more radical. They query the whole purpose of the system, whether it should exist at all. They are not concerned with their own personal adjustment to the system until they have established whether the system should be in existence in the first place. Clearly "how" questions are a mark of tranquil times when established truths and institutions are running smoothly without being seriously challenged. Characteristic of such times are a concern with fairly minute questions about forms of procedure and personal examination of worthiness to belong to the institution; there is an atmosphere about them of peace and almost complacency. Everything is going well without great changes; most people are happy, at least in a superficial way. By contrast the times when people are questioning not "how" but "whether" are far from tranquil and give peace to no one — unless he is a man who has faced the challenge of asking the radical questions and not run away from the answers he gets but acted honestly according to his findings. Those who in a time of radical questioning do not face these queries but try to postpone them or pretend they are not serious, find themselves living haunted lives with no peace and recurring anxiety. At a time of radical questions there is no peace for the man who does not make himself ask them. For instance, in a time when indissoluble marrige is accepted without question married couples find it easy to stay married, and ask "how" questions about their life together: how they should adjust to each other, how they should face the future. The result is peace and complacency. At a time, however, when indissoluble marriage is not accepted everywhere but greatly questioned with divorce a possibility for all, married people will inevitably ask "whether" questions about their marriage, so that even minor tiffs can be occasions of serious questioning about the suitability of staying together. This is clearly a much more anxious and less tranquil kind of life to live. But it is one that brings a more radical peace in the end, for the couples that have had the courage to face these radical questions about themselves and have worked through to a solution will achieve an understanding of each other at a deeper level than before. Their life together will be ultimately more secure after facing the "whether" question than if they had only asked the "how" question. And there will be no danger now of complacency. They have faced the deeper issues together and have penetrated to the heart of marriage. Their questioning has brought them wisdom.

It is no secret that the times we live in are supremely a time of "whether" questions. In every institution in the land and every department of life men are asking "whether" questions, and once asked these questions cannot be refused an answer! It is no doubt highly inconvenient that we should be asking ourselves these awkward questions and we often wish we did not have to, but the fact is that all these questions are being asked by someone and at least some are rising in our own minds, and they cannot be answered by being ignored. The consequent anxiety and loss of peace is the price of being born in a time of radical change in society. Thus with regard to the State, the Party System, the Monarchy, the Army, the Democratic way of life, Capitalism; we are asking not how they should be conducted and organized in the present age but whether they should exist at all. The result is an atmosphere of intellectual turmoil, which depending on temperament can be regarded as exciting or depressing, but which is certainly not boring.

Because the Church is part of mankind and is (thank goodness) in step with the deepest aspirations of men, christians too are living in a time of radical questioning and intellectual turmoil. The change has been most marked in the last decade, especially in the Catholic Church which is entering upon a time of anxious "whether" questions after an unprecedented period of tranquillity and complacency when the only questions that bothered us were "how" questions. A glance at any religious journal in 1960 and again in 1970 will show how very changed are the problems which concern the reading Catholic. Then, it was *how,* now it is the *whether,* that exercises us about christianity. You can take almost any accepted thing in the Catholic Church and notice that the manner of its being dealt with has changed. The Priesthood — not how priests should live but what a priest is, is now the question. Complusory Celibacy — ten years ago we searched into ways of being faithful to the promise of celibacy that all priests made, now we ask whether there should be such a promise. The loyal parishioner — we no longer ask how to be one, but question whether the parish system is a good one. And so on through all the traditional "given" things in the Church, from the infallible Pope in Rome to the devotional life of a Catholic. As can be seen from this book, the practice of prayer itself is questioned rather than the way it is done. This is what living in radical times means: a constant questioning of the existence of things in the Church before any attempt can be made to settle down to them and make them work. Once again, of course, it is the man who runs away from asking these radical questions who is the loser and who never has a moment's peace. (That too can be seen from the pages of our religious journals.) The man who, on the contrary, courageously faces the radical questions and who, however inadequate he may feel about his ability to find solutions alone, nevertheless continues to try to make his faith authentic by pursuing these questions is the man who wins. It is not an easy victory. It would not be a truly christian pursuit if it was. Those, however, who have undertaken the questioning search for authentic faith in today's Church and World have the reward of a living faith which really does mean something to them since it has become the deepest principle by which they live. The exciting thing about christianity today is that this growth is taking place in so many people. Where before the christian yes led few people existentially to the ultimate questions and so only a few were faced with the awful choice between atheism and belief, now many are finding that the initial yes of their christian response is leading them with uncomfortable speed to the ultimate questions from which true faith springs. A radical time is producing radical issues and radical anxieties are giving birth to deep faith among christians today. There is no room for complacent acceptance now and the conformist christian whose faith is no more than a following of the social pattern (and consequently not faith at all) is becoming rarer.

The ultimate question that every follower of Christ has to ask, behind all the questions about Church and Family and Christian Living, is the question about God. Not how we should acknowledge him, but whether he exists. This is the last "whether" question that is eventually reached by the radical questioner, and when he reaches it he finds that it is also the first question, because all the other christian questions depend on the answer to this one. It would be silly to be bothered about whether or not to lead a christian family life if God did not exist, to take a plain example. It is to this question "Does God exist?" that the christian affirmation eventually leads. If we remain open to God through all the problems of life and go on facing the questions that are posed to us without running away (i.e., if we go on growing) then sooner or later we are challenged by this last/first question which can only be answered by an act of faith. The problems of love and the problems of hope involved in being a christian in the world depend on this problem of faith. When we face that problem and in faith remain open to God we are already in principle answering the subsequent problems of hope and love which are contained in trying to be a christian in today's world. The question of faith is the one that first matters.

In the ages of christendom when christianity was not deeply questioned but was the accepted background to all life, the radical question of faith was faced by few people — only those whose response to God had taken them far in his service. For St. John of the Cross, for instance, the trials of faith as opposed to the trials of the senses were undergone only by the few who reached his Night of the Spirit.[1] The experience today is that even ordinary christians, provided they are sincere, find themselves up against the trials of faith early in their service of God. These trials are not today a phenomenon of "advanced" christians but of ordinary christian living. This is because the atmosphere of radical questioning which all christians

In St. John of the Cross's scheme the Night of the senses corresponds to the "how" questions of christian living and the Night of the Spirit corresponds to the "whether" questions.

158

breathe daily leads them to the "whether" questions at the same time as the "how" questions. Paradoxically people are undergoing the trials of the spirit before and during the lesser trials of adjusting themselves to christian living. The old fixed patterns of christian spirituality are no longer accurate representations of what is happening.

It is difficult to give helpful advice about the trials of faith we are asked by Christ to undergo. When our trial is one of how to be a christian we can be advised to hold firmly to our trust and faith in God the Father in the midst of the ruin of our former spiritual edifice. By doing this we grow out of dependence on "religion" and grow deeper in faith, which is our direct link with the Father in whose care we live and move and have our being. It is a trying time, but the reward is a deeper confidence and faith in God, now experienced as a living Force in our lives. It is a growth point of faith. But when the foundation of our faith is itself in question and we are left without that support in life, because we are now doubting (with so many others) if God exists at all, then there is nothing left in our lives to cling to and therefore nothing to write about. At the heart of our being is a great emptiness, a great question mark. We were assured that the journey inward would lead us to the Trinity dwelling within us, but now we are not certain of that. All that we can do is *wait* in complete emptiness. In this way our whole lives, busy about ordinary things from morning to night as we earn our daily bread and keep our family going, become an experience of waiting. We can no longer go through the motions of hoping and trusting in God as he appeared to us before we doubted, so we in emptiness wait. It has been well put by the poet:

> I said to my soul, be still, and wait without hope
> For hope would be hope for the wrong thing; wait
> without love
> For love would be love of the wrong thing; there
> is yet faith
> But the faith and the love and the hope are all in
> the waiting.
> Wait without thought, for you are not ready for
> thought:
> So the darkness shall be the light, and the stillness
> the dancing.

(T. S. Eliot: East Coker)

The stage when a christian doubts whether God exists and consequently does not know how to continue his christian affirmation, and yet carries on saying yes in the darkness, is the stage when it is granted to him to grasp the presence of the sacred in the midst of the secular. We have seen how the presence of mystery in the physical world is on the way to being abolished by the forces of secularism in our modern technological age. But we also saw that this did not mean that Mystery was no longer present in the world. What it meant was that we have learned to look for Mystery in the proper place, not in the physical realm but in the realm of ultimate purpose, the world which undergirds the physical world and which is discovered by pursuing "whether" questions about life. There Mystery is discovered, not fast disappearing but present as crucially as ever. This is the presence of God, the triune mystery of Father, Son and Holy Spirit, by which the world is created and given meaning. The follower of Christ who has been led by his faith to penetrate to these ultimate problems is thus able to encounter the sacred element in life and know it existentially as a baffling mystery. Such a man knows from experience that the mysterious purpose of God's salvation is at work in the world, and that in spite of man's astonishing discoveries which are removing mystery from the scientific world, the deepest meaning of the universe is still completely beyond his grasp. He is thus at

home with the mysterious sacred as an element at the heart of the secular, and finds
himself able to move at ease between the
two, because he knows that they are two
sides of the same coin. To know this is to
have wisdom. Wisdom is a gift from the
Father which is learned only with suffering,
the suffering of doubting the foundations of
one's faith. But wisdom is also what the
world needs most. So we can take heart that
the radical questioning which is upsetting
our former peace and complacency is leading us to a deeper understanding of the
meaning of the universe, and making us pro-
foundly useful members of society. In this
way, saying yes to people which leads us in
faith to say yes to God the Father leads us
back to saying yes to people and society,
and the circle is completed.